Research Methods in English

Research Methods in English

M.P. Sinha

ATLANTIC
PUBLISHERS & DISTRIBUTORS (P) LTD

ATLANTIC
PUBLISHERS & DISTRIBUTORS (P) LTD
7/22, Ansari Road, Darya Ganj, New Delhi
Tel.: +91-11-4077 5252, 2327 3880
E-mail: orders@atlanticbooks.com
Web: www.atlanticbooks.com

Reprint 2026

Published by Atlantic Publishers & Distributors (P) Ltd.

Printed & bound in India by Atlantic Print Services

Preface

The main aim of the book is to introduce the methods and techniques of research in English literature to M.A., M.Phil. and Ph.D. students. In India, literary research is still confined to the interpretation and evaluation of a creative writer. In England and America it covers a much wider range and includes such areas as editing of texts, determination of authenticity and chronology, interpretation of literary terms, history of ideas and biography.

Now that we have established authors like Aurobindo Ghosh, Sarojini Naidu, Toru Dutt, R.K. Narayan, Raja Rao, Mulk Raj Anand and many others, it will be really a fruitful research activity to edit their texts and determine their chronology. The day is not far away when we shall apply all the methods and techniques of research being applied in England and America and produce definitive editions and standard biographies.

Secondly, a large number of research students do not define their critical stance and this is because they have not read modern theories of literature. Naturally, their analysis and interpretation of literary texts is usually muddled. To make them aware of the concepts in modern criticism, a brief summary of the main features of the more important critical theories is given in the chapter entitled *Methods*.

Thirdly, the chapters "The Literary Thesis" and "Bibliographical References" will help students in collecting material and writing theses or doctoral dissertations in a more planned way.

The book is not exhaustive and the researcher is advised to consult Richard D. Altick's *The Art of Literary Research*, Chauncey Sanders's *An Introduction to Research in Literary History*, *MLA Handbook for the Writers of Research Papers* and *Thesis* and *Assignment Writing*. The last two books are available in paperback edition.

I am thankful to my wife Veena Sinha for her encouragement and help, and to Dr. K.R. Gupta, Chairman, Atlantic Publishers and Distributors, New Delhi, for printing it immaculately in a short time.

M.P. SINHA

Contents

1

Meaning and Objectives of Literary Research

Meaning of Research

There is a difference between "skimming" and "reading." "Skimming" connotes hurried reading. We usually skim a newspaper. Reading refers to thoroughness. Editorials and lead articles are read, not skimmed. Study is intensive reading. We read a novel or a short story in general. But we study, when we have to review or make comments on them. Research is more than study; it has assumed a new meaning in the twentieth century. The Old French word *cerchier* (Latin *circare*) meant "to go about." The English word search nowadays means to survey inquiringly or to examine or inspect closely. The word research has been coined by the addition of the prefix "re" such as we have in words like reunite, remake, redo, re-organise and retell. The word research originally had the same connotation as the words reunite and redo mean today. But now it is purely a technical term. It means a systematic investigation in a field of knowledge to discover or establish facts or principles. It also means a fresh approach to a subject or interpretation of facts. The following definitions will give us a clear idea what research is :

1. [Research is] "a systematic investigation for the purpose of gaining new knowledge. In a broad sense, research is any study that leads to new knowledge for the person doing research." (New Standard Encyclopedia)

2. [Research is] "a search or investigation directed to the discovery of some fact by careful consideration or study of a subject, a course of critical or scientific inquiry."

(Oxford English Dictionary)

3. [Research is] "a studious inquiry or examination; especially critical and exhaustive investigation or experimentation having for its aim the discovery of new facts and their correct information, the revision of accepted conclusions, theories, or laws in the light of newly discovered facts, or the practical applications of such new or revised conclusions, theories or laws."

(Webster's International Dictionary)

A close reading of these definitions will lead us to the conclusion that research has the following features :

(a) Research is a systematic and critical investigation.

(b) It aims at the discovery of new facts and their correct information.

(c) It is also the revision of accepted laws or theories in the light of the discovery of new facts.

(d) It can be the practical application of new or revised conclusions, theories or laws.

Coming to the first feature, the word systematic means that the entire procedure of the investigation is done under certain principles. The word critical means that the researcher takes care of both kinds of facts, one that favours his hypothesis and the other that goes counter to his assumptions. It follows then, that the researcher must not be prejudiced or subjective in his observation, experiment, analysis or interpretation nor should he be erratic in the arrangement of facts nor ignore the facts that shatter his postulates or hypothesis. Suppose a researcher assumes that Hopkins is purely a modern poet and is entirely different from the other Victorians. Now if he finds that Hopkins is Victorian in his attitude and ideas, he must not ignore this fact and must revise his hypothesis.

Secondly, research should be a genuine contribution to knowledge. This is possible only when we discover a new fact or interpret a known fact in a new way. We all know that Shakespeare has written thirty-six plays. Suppose someone comes with a manuscript and systematically proves it to be the playwright's thirty-seventh play, he has discovered a new fact and made a genuine contribution to knowledge. Likewise Caroline Spurgeon's interpretation of Shakespeare's imagery is a new kind of interpretation and hence a genuine contribution to knowledge.

Thirdly, research is also that kind of investigation which examines an accepted theory to revise or modify or sometimes reject it. Copernicus examined the old concept of the universe, found it unacceptable, and after rejecting it posited his new concept. Likewise the linguists of the seventeenth century considered Latin and Greek to be the most ancient languages. Later on, Sir William Jones, after his arrival in India and study of Sanskrit, propounded that Sanskrit was the most ancient language and all the European and, Indian languages have their origin in it. But this theory too, he revised and modified later on. Now the accepted theory is that the Indian and European languages have their source in Proto-Indo-European language.

Finally, research can be of applied kind. Here the investigator applies the abstract principles of a theory for practical purposes. Einstein's theory of relativity is applied in space research. In literature, Freud's psychology is being applied in the analysis of a literary text. Chomsky's transformational generative grammar is being applied in computers.

Literary Research

Uptill now we have discussed research in general. But the nature of research differs from subject to subject. This is because materials and tools of each subject are largely different. Physics, chemistry, botany, zoology and other natural sciences study natural phenomena. Their basic tools are observation and experiment. They replicate the natural conditions in the laboratory and observe the changes minutely. The social sciences study man and his behaviour. But man cannot be put in a laboratory to be experimented on in the way natural objects can be. Naturally, observation and interview are the important tools that we use in social sciences. Secondly, the experiments of science can be repeated but this is rather difficult in social sciences and humanities, excepting psychology and linguistics.

Literature is different from natural sciences or social sciences. It is the product of the creative writer. Literary research, therefore, cannot confine itself to either the literary text or the writer; it has to study both. When its material (the object of study) is the creative writer, it applies the tools of social sciences and when the object of study is the text, it applies the tools which are specific to it. But it will be rash to separate these two aspects of literary research. While studying the text we cannot ignore its creator nor can we study an author isolating him from his works. The other important fact we have to bear in mind is that the methods of analysis and evaluation of a literary text have become autonomous. They have their own theories and principles which are being constantly modified and revised.

In natural sciences and social sciences we have two kinds of research : basic and applied. Literary Research, because of the duality of its object of study, is of four kinds : (a) Bibliography and textual criticism, (b) Biographical, (c) Theoretical and (d) Interpretive.

(a) Bibliography and Textual Criticism. Textual research is concerned with the establishment of an authoritative text, correction of past editions, chronology, authenticity and attribution. No reader can appreciate a text which is full of errors. Secondly, he must know that the text he is reading is a genuine one. Critics have been misled by printing errors or faulty texts F.O. Mathiessen's interpretation of the phrase "soiled fish of the sea" in Melville's *white Jacket* fell flat when it was discovered that the word is "coiled," not "soiled." Similarly F.R. Leavis's praise of Henry James's *Roderick Hudson* became ludicrous when scholars pointed out that he had read the revised edition, not the original edition. In order that an author be read as he had written and his works be presented in a chronological order, it is necessary to produce reliable texts. In modern times definitive editions are prepared in the personal supervision of the author but in the past it was not so. If we study the sixteenth, seventeenth or eighteenth or even nineteenth century editions, we will find striking variations.

In modern times, this kind of research has gained more importance. Now we know the difference between Shakespeare's bad quarto and good folio, the forgerers of the nineteenth century and the pirated editions of Charles Dickens. Again most of the important authors have left some of their works unpublished, which when combined with the published material, give us a different picture of them.

(b) **Biographical.** This kind of research, though neglected in India, is of first importance in the understanding of an author's mind and art. The task of the biographer is really very difficult. All biographers are not fortunate like Boswell. A biographer has to collect material from different sources, study the author's published works and unpublished writings as well, interview him frequently if he is alive, meet and collect information from the people close to him, distinguish fact from fiction and after that present the life story, laying more emphasis on the literary side by correlating the important events of his life and time and his works, systematically, chronologically and interestingly.

(c) **Theoretical.** This kind of research can be compared to the basis research in natural and social sciences. Its aim is to propound a theory of literature or modify and improve an already existing one. In the past after Aristotle and Longinus, few scholars and philosophers took literary criticism seriously. They often repeated the classical theory of literature. In England, theoretical criticism was left to poets only. But Sidney, Dryden and Pope cannot be said to be original in their approach. Coleridge and Wordsworth were the first to propound a theory of literature and were ably followed by Matthew Arnold. In the twentieth century, advances in psychology, anthropology, linguistics and sociology made people to look at literature from quite different angles. The modern critics have defined their approach, method and technique and analysed literary texts and evaluated creative writers on the basis of the theories they have formulated after a wide range of study. Now, we have different schools of criticism like New Criticism, Myth Criticism, Hermeneutic Criticism, Psycho-analytic Criticism, Marxist Criticism, Structuralism and Deconstruction, Feminist Criticism, Post-colonial theory and new historicism and cultural materialism, all systematic and distinct.

(d) **Interpretive.** This kind of research can be compared to the applied research in sciences. It analyses, interprets and evaluates a literary text of an author by applying the principles of a particular theory. It may be a study of an author's style, use of imagery or symbolism, exploration of myth, perception of social reality, expression of the inner soul, development of thought or the structure of his texts. What is important in this kind of research is the systematicity in the use of the principles and use of both inductive and deductive methods. The researcher must not assume that the text would behave as he would wish. A literary text is *sui generis*. It can not be a replica of the other. Naturally, the researcher has to modify his methods and techniques occasionally and sometimes to revise the theory he has adopted.

Although it has been discussed that there are four kinds of research, a scholar cannot ignore anyone of them. Interpretive research is closely linked with the theoretical research. The editor of a text must be able to interpret the text; otherwise he cannot collate and emend it. The biographer carries the tasks of both the editor and critic. In short literary research is a composite whole and a researcher must know all its aspects. It is only when he chooses a special field that he does biographical, textual, theoretical or interpretive research.

Aims and Objectives of Research

The university education system has three main functions : (a) teaching, (b) research and (c) extension. The first function, teaching is handing down the torch of knowledge to the next generation. Close down all the educational institutions for eighty years and you will see that the entire nation has receded to its pre-historic age. It will be inhabited by the ignorant, barbaric, uncivilised people. Teaching is the most important function because without it the younger generation will never have access to the treasure of knowledge its forefathers have collected. Research adds something new to the treasure of knowledge and without it teaching will lose its utility gradually. If teaching went on repeating what is already known and ignoring the new knowledge acquired by research, civilisation would not progress. A conscientious teacher always learns something new, makes it a part of the storage of his knowledge, modifies his views in the light of new facts, reorders his methods and goes to the classroom to acquaint the learners with the new knowledge he has gained. In other words he is engaged in research. He is never satisfied with the knowledge that he possesses; his thirst to know more is never quenched and he will never limit himself to repeating the old things in the classroom every year. He is eager that his students would do those things which he has not been able to do or had no time to do.

Literary research has four main objectives :

(a) Advancement of knowledge,

(b) Broadening the mind and sharpening the critical insight of the researcher,

(c) Creation of a genuine and intelligent interest in literature,

(d) Inculcation of the sense that the researcher is a member of a collaborative community.

(a) Advancement of knowledge. There are two aspects of it The first is the assimilation of the intellectual achievements of the predecessors. Research means going from the known to the unknown. It is necessary that the researcher should have a thorough knowledge of what has been done in the past and what the present status of knowledge in the field of his investigation is. If he wants to do research on Milton, for instance, he must study not only all the works of the poet but also the views of different critics from the time of Milton to the present day.* If he does not do so, there is every possibility that he will repeat the ideas that have already been expressed. A.C. Bradley, before advancing his explanation that melancholy was the cause of Hamlet's delay, examined the explanations given by different critics. The researcher, therefore, should first survey the literature on the topic he is going to do research. For this, he must study the different points of view disinterestedly and critically, and assimilate logically for full understanding of the problem he is going to investigate.

The second aspect is the discovery of new facts and a fresh interpretation of the known facts. C.S. Chandrashekhar's discovery of the black hole is the result of his research. Similarly the discovery of radium by the Curies was a genuine contribution to knowledge. In science old theories have been frequently revised in the light of new facts or fresh interpretations have been made after a more scientific analysis

* Generally, there is the survey of literature that precedes the main body of the thesis.

of the known facts. Earlier it was believed that heavier things fell on the earth with greater velocity than the lighter ones. The typical example was the dropping of a coin and a feather. Later on, further experiments proved that all things fall with the same velocity. The previous scientists did not notice the resistance of air. The resistance of air was much less in the case of a metal coin than that of a feather. It was the resistance of air that prevented the feather from falling with the velocity of the coin. When both were dropped in a vacuum, they fell at the same time.

If we simply describe or repeat what other people have done, we will be teachers but never research scholars. In our survey of literature we must refer to both the positive and negative points of our predecessors, correct their ideas and advance our own explanation of the facts that were either overlooked or wrongly observed and interpreted by them, and avoid being a mediocre narrator. It is only the genuineness and originality of interpretation which makes our research a contribution to the total body of knowledge. Donne, though a great seventeenth century poet, did not receive his due recognition till Sir Herbert Grierson edited his poetry and wrote a long introduction pointing out his great qualities. It was his interpretation of Donne and other metaphysical poets that drew the attention of T.S. Eliot, F.R. Leavis and other poets and critics who placed these poets in the front rank. G. Wilson Knight's interpretation of Shakespeare's plays opened a new vista. Jon Stollworthy's study of different drafts of Yeats's important poems and analysis of the development of his thought at each stage has widened our knowledge of the great Irish poet.

(b) Broadening the mind and sharpening the critical insight of the researcher. The researcher is made of a different stuff. An average reader goes through a novel, a play or a poem for two reasons : (i) entertainment and (ii) morals. He seldom bothers about the artistic presentation of reality. He may react against the views expressed in a book or disbelieve the facts presented there. He does so, because the contents of the book go against the ideas he has held uptill now. Research warns us of such kind of reading. What Bacon said in the seventeenth century is still valid for a researcher.

"Read not to contradict and confute, nor to believe and

take for granted, nor to find talk and discourse, but to weigh and consider" ("Of Studies").

In order that we can properly study a book we should not read to find in it what we already know nor to confirm our opinion already formed but to observe the facts stated there and analyse the author's view and compare them with our own. For this, there is the necessity of critical insight.

How to develop our critical insight? How to avoid being gullible or credulous? This can be done by wide reading and participation in seminars and symposia. By wide reading we mean study of life and literature in not only the chosen field but also other disciplines. Life is complex. The different branches of knowledge — physics, chemistry, biology, medicine, economics, anthropology, religion, politics, history etc. study man's different aspects and behaviours. It may be said that natural sciences study nature and the universe, not man. But, in fact, science studies nature and the universe in relation to man; all its investigations are directed to solve his problems.

Since literature, which is an expression of man's problems and aspirations, studies man in all walks of life, it influences and in turn, is influenced by all the branches of knowledge. Naturally, the researcher cannot develop a critical insight unless and until he has an elementary knowledge of the natural sciences, social sciences, philosophy, history and religion. A creative writer welds all the knowledge he has gained in his imaginative work. Milton made use of Ptolemy's concept of the universe, Chaucer of astrology, and Donne his knowledge of science. In modern times poets and novelists have a much wider range. For example, Eliot based his *Waste Land* on Jessie Weston's *From Ritual to Romance* and Sir James Frazer's *The Golden Borgh* and the poets of nineteen thirties made use of the ideas of Freud and Marx.

Secondly, the young researcher must be able to make distinction between a good text and a bad text. Most of bazaar editions of Shakespeare are full of errors. It will be a good exercise to compare the critical editions of Shakespeare with the Indian bazaar editions. A reliable text saves us from the pitfalls of misinterpretation. The cases of Mathiessen and Leavis have already been cited.

Thirdly, we must develop the ability to evaluate and judge the general reliability of published research. All critics are not impartial. Their judgments are warped by their postulates, methods, faulty application and personal prejudices. For the postulates, we cannot blame a critic. His theory of literature is both his strength and limit A historical critic like Hyppolite-Taine would not analyse a text in detail like the New Critic. What is important for us is to know the difference between their approaches and find out whether they have followed their methods logically; only a mature scholar-critic can analyse the strength and weakness of their approaches.

We must know why F.R. Leavis and the early Eliot denounced Milton and why the later Eliot praised him. It is important to know why Dr. Johnson criticised Milton's pastoral poems unfavourably, and think whether he was right in his judgment. It is interesting to read R.S. Crane's criticism of Cleanth Brooks's method and Dr. Leavis's pronouncement made in *The Great Tradition* that after Shakespeare there are only four poets worth reading : Donne, Hopkins, Pound and Eliot. In short, we must not take it for granted that all that is printed in a book is correct or that all British and American critics are always right in their approach and technique or that Indian critics are inferior to them. We should use the evaluation procedure* to judge the merit of published research and criticism.

(c) Creation of a genuine and intelligent interest in literature. People go to a man of learning for knowledge. If a scholar fails to help people gain knowledge, he will never get respect and honour; rather people will call him an impostor, a humbug. Therefore the aim of literary research is to create in the young researcher a genuine interest in literature. Research is something more than earning a qualification or fame. It is an activity which is a reward in itself. The aim of research is

---

* Noam Chomsky criticised the discovery procedure of the structural linguists and advocated for evaluation procedure which means that the linguist should evaluate two grammars, say A and B, on the basis of their explanation of the rules of a language. The grammar which gives a more satisfactory explanation is better than the other. We can say that of the two critics or the two approaches, that one is better which better explains the structure of a text or the entire work of an author.

to develop the powers of understanding and appreciating literature. An average reader is satisfied with whatever is presented to him. He will not bother why one literary text is superior to the other. But a researcher, because he has developed his powers of understanding and appreciating, is able to explain why George Eliot is superior to Maugham. He is confident in his analysis because he has read literature with genuine interest, developed his critical insight and analysed both the novelists systematically. Since he has developed an insight in literature, he is self-reliant and he need not look for other critics' judgment at every stage of his analysis and may logically refute their judgment if he feels genuinely so.

(d) Research creates a sense of belongingness to a collaborative community. Research is a collective responsibility shared by all researchers. Besides, it is not limited to time. Every generation carries on the task which was not completed by the previous generation. Some of the problems that were left by Copernicus were completed by Galileo. Nowadays research is so widespread that it is not limited to a university or even a country. We see scientists from different countries receive Nobel Prize for working on the same topic.

In literature, too, we must be aware of the fact that there are thousands of scholars like us. We all belong to a community which is dedicated to the enrichment of culture, to better understanding of man's feelings, emotions and problems through literature and to creation of an ideal environment in the university where we are working. We can conclude in the words of Dr. F.R. Leavis :

"Research should be able to generate in the university a centre of human consciousness, perception, knowledge, judgment and responsibility. Research has to be thought of in relation to the whole idea of university. It must aim at establishing a creative front and doing creative work on the contemporary intellectual frontier."[1]

NOTE

1. Leavis, F.R., *English Literature in Our Time and the University,* (London : CUP, 1967).

2

Background Knowledge

Research in a university is possible with a proper understanding between the researcher and the supervisor. The supervisor selects a candidate to work with him mainly on two considerations : aptitude and background knowledge. It is expected that the research student shall have the following qualities.

(a) **Dedication to Learning.** First and foremost the student must not think of material gains. Money and fame may be the by-products of research but never its aim. In *Murder in the Cathedral* Thomas Becket considers the Fourth Tempter the worst because it lures him to martyrdom for fame. A martyr, according to Becket, sacrifices his life for the suffering humanity, not for personal gain. The research scholar, too, dedicates his life to learning for the benefit of mankind, for the advancement of knowledge, for the discovery of truth. He does research for the love of it. Charles Lamb wrote in "Old China" that it was really arduous and painful to pass through the crowd to reach the gallery of the theatre where the plays of Shakespeare were staged. But once he reached the gallery and found a seat there and the curtain was raised, he forgot all the troubles he had suffered on the way :

> "...and when the curtain drew up, what cared we for our place in the house, or what mattered it where we were sitting, when our thoughts were with Rosalind in Arden, or with Viola at the Court of Illyria?"

The research student should forget everything when he is engaged in research. He should feel happy that his research on an author or age or a text will be a contribution to knowledge.

(b) Scepticism. The research scholar should be sceptic in his investigation. He must not take everything at its face value. He should be aware of the fact that man is fallible and no scholar, however great, is free from error. Richard D. Altick has quoted a number of examples of forgerers and story-tellers.[1] His illustrations and comments make it amply clear that authors, their friends and critics are not always reliable. They sometimes conceal facts, concoct stories, make mistakes in dates, deprecate their rivals and enemies and occasionally give second hand information. We all know now that Shakespeare came from a respectable middle class family, that he was well-educated and that he deliberately chose his profession. But because Ben Jonson was envious of him, he remarked that Shakespeare knew little Latin and less Greek. The false opinion that Shakespeare was not properly educated or even educated continued till the end of the nineteenth century. It is the modern biographers who after checking the Church and school records exploded the myth that he was "nature's child." Similarly, a biographer romanticised his story by saying that he fled away from Stratford-on-Avon because he was convicted for poaching. Now we all know that this story has nothing to do with the Bard of Avon.[2]

(c) Command of language. A text is essentially a linguistic structure. A creative writer presents his perception of reality through the medium of language. The reader, too, tries to understand the author's presentation of reality by analysing the language of the text. In order that he can understand the text rightly he must have a good command of language. English contains a very large number of words. It is expected that a student of B.A. should have the active vocabulary of 5,000 words and of M.A. about 8,000 words. A research student should know at least 10,000 words. If he has a poor vocabulary, he will face difficulty at every stage. Besides, many words in English have undergone semantic change. Words like fool, sweet, wife and train had different meanings in the seventeenth century. In one of his sonnets Shakespeare wrote : "O train me not...."

Here the word "train" means "tempt." In Herbert's poem "Virtue" the word "sweets" means perfume. I still remember that my teacher while explaining the poem gave us the modern meaning of the word.

The meaning of a sentence is not the sum total of the meanings of its words. It is the structure, ordering of words and their relationship, that determines the meaning of a sentence. For example, we can take these two sentences.

(i) He was a great man.

(ii) A great man he was.

Both the sentences have the same words but differ in meaning because of the difference in structure. Poets and playwrights always break the norms of convention for desired effects. They coin new words, make experiments with structure and sometimes deliberately produce ambiguity.

Finally, the researcher has not only to read but also to write clearly and lucidly. It is expected that he will write both correctly and appropriately. He is advised to keep a good dictionary that can help him use the right word. The best dictionary for Indian students is *Advanced Learners' Dictionary* which gives meaning of words and their usage. The other good dictionary is *Webster's New Dictionary and Thesaurus.* The third handy dictionary is *Oxford Etymological Dictionary* which gives the meaning of words and their origin. For building word power he should read *Reader's Digest* regularly. The magazine gives 20 words in each of its issue to increase the word power of the reader. *Forum,* a journal published in the USA but available in India also, is useful for both students and teachers of English. The special quality of this journal is that the meaning of difficult words and expressions in each article is given at the end in a box.

It is a false assumption, and this is quite common, of the students of English literature that while doing research they should read books of literature only. The fact is that all branches of knowledge have converged again. Now literature is so wide in scope that it is studied seriously by all people. People from different disciplines write plays, poems and novels. They also express their views of literature. Bronowski, an authority on William Blake, was one of the top scientists of England. Joseph Conrad was a sea-captain. Isaac Asimov was a physicist. A student of literature, now, cannot afford to remain aloof from other branches of knowledge and shut himself away in the tower of "pure" literature. A thorough knowledge of the following is essential for him before he ventures to do research :

(a) Social and Intellectual Background.

(b) Major Literary Movements.

(c) Approaches to Literature.

(d) Classical Literature and Ancient Myths.

Besides, a working knowledge of the following is desirable :

(e) Linguistics.

(f) Psychology.

(g) Christianity.

(h) Sociology.

(a) Social and intellectual background. Literature is primarily a social product and the poet is a member of a society. In spite of all his individuality he represents his social group. This social group has its own ideas and philosophy. For a full understanding of his works it is necessary to study the social conditions and dominant ideas of his time. If we want to study Shakespeare seriously, we first should know the kind of people the Elizabethans were, their custom, their beliefs, their way of life, the relationship between different social groups and the dominant ideas of the sixteenth and seventeenth century England.

The changes in the social structure caused by the changes in the economic structure are responsible for the emergence of new ideas. People of the new age do not think like the people of the preceding age. Before the renaissance the European society was controlled by kings and priests. The middle class had no control over the means of production. People believed in the divine rights of the king and considered the Pope a representative of God. The rise of the middle class made people think in a new way. The old philosophy gave way to new philosophy, humanism took the place of divinity. Feudalism began to gave way to democracy and the focus shifted from the aristocracy to the middle class. In Shakespeare's plays there is the description of a hierarchical society in which the king is at the top and the serf is at the bottom. But in Milton it is not so; there is a challenge to authority and this is because feudalism was challenged by the middle class under the leadership of Cromwell. G.M. Trevelyan's *Illustrated Social History of England* is a good introduction to the social background and Basil Willey's *Seventeenth Century Background, Eighteenth Century Background, Nineteenth Century Background* and *More Nineteenth Century Studies* are the best studies on the intellectual background. *The Pelican Guide* has a chapter, the "Social Scene," at the beginning of each of its volume.

(b) **Literary movement.** The social conditions provide content and the intellectual movements ideas to a literary work but it is the literary movements that are responsible for the artistic expression. In every age, due to the changes in social conditions and emergence of new ideas, writers have experimented with the forms and language for desired expression. The different genres of literature, the different forms of poetry, drama, novel and essay and the different stanza forms and metre forms are result of the writers' experiment. A great writer is a vital link in the entire chain of literary history. He studies the merits and drawbacks of his predecessors, views the present reality and makes experiments with language, and forms of literature. For his proper evaluation or his age it is profitable to know the periods that preceded and followed his age. Eliot has rightly said that no poet, no artist has his meaning alone.

B. Ifor Evans's *A short History of English Literature* and Emile Legouis' *A short History of English Literature* are good introductions. The other books a research student should consult are the monumental *Cambridge History of English Literature, Oxford History of English Literature, A Literary History of England, A Literary History of America* and Legouis and Cazamian's *A History of English Literature.*

(c) **Approaches to Literature.** The quality of a text can be judged through an objective analysis based on a theory. A theory is a set of principles formulated after the analysis of a large number of texts; the procedure is always inductive. Aristotle's *Poetics* propounds a theory of literature and so do Richards's *Principles of Literary Criticism* and *Practical Criticism.* An analysis which is not based on a theory is bound to be subjective and confusing.[3]

Now modern criticism is so divergent and fast changing that no research student can be able to master all the theories or approaches of criticism. He has already read Aristotle, Longinus, Sidney, Dryden, Coleridge, Wordsworth, Arnold and a few modern critics. He is now advised to study New Criticism, Neo-Aristotelians, Psycho-analytic criticism, Myth Criticism, Marxist Criticism, Structuralism, Feminist Criticism and if possible, Deconstruction. A knowledge of these different schools of criticism and their critical stance will help him understand the modern critics and choose his own approach to an author or a text. He can study any one of these Readers :

1. Scott, Wilbur. *Five Approaches of Criticism.* New York : Macmillan, 1962.

2. Handy, William J. and Max Westbrook. *Twentieth Century Criticism.* Delhi : Light & Life Publishers, 1976.

3. Lodge, David. *Twentieth Century Criticism.* London : Longman, 1972.

However, it will be of great value to him if he reads all the three. The new anthology of modern criticism entitled *Modern Criticism and Theory* (1988) edited by David Lodge and published by Longman includes essays on Structuralism, Post-structuralism and Deconstruction. Rene Wellek's *A History of Modern Criticism* in 7 volumes is the best survey. The other good books on the history of criticism are David Daiches's *Critical Approaches to Literature* and Wimsatt and Brooks's *Literary Criticism : A Short History,* both available in cheap editions.

(d) Classical literature and ancient myths. English literature, though one of the richest in the world, does not have a long history. The poets of the sixteenth and seventeenth centuries did not have any English epics nor mythology that could give them material for their poetry and drama. They were not in the happy position of the Indian poets who inherited a rich mythology and the two great epics the *Ramayana* and the *Mahabharata* that provided them material for their poetry. The English poets naturally had to look for models. The renaissance helped them in their search. It was through the Italian scholars that the English people came to know about Homer's *Iliad* and *Odyssey,* the plays of Aeschylus, Sophocles and Euripedes,

Aristotle's *Poetics,* Virgil's *Aeneid,* Dante's *Divine Comedy* and Longinus' *On the Sublime.* The introduction of the classical Greek and Latin literature had a tremendous impact on the English writers. They made experiments on the different forms of literature, used the Greek and Latin source materials in their poems and plays and followed, sometimes loosely and in general strictly, the classical principles of poetics, and profusely made use of the Greek and Roman mythology. The trend that started in the sixteenth century is still continuing. We can say that English literature is a continuance of the ancient Greek and Latin literatures.

Myths are a useful means to link the past with the present. They are used to prove that man in spite of all his progress in science is basically the same being he was thousands of years ago. Since mythical figures symbolise the aspirations of the community, especially the quest myth figures, poets have imaged them to symbolise their individual aspiration as well as of their community. Prometheus, for example, is a saviour of mankind in Shelley's *Prometheus Unbound.*

Because England and America do not have their own mythology, except that of king Arthur, English writers naturally had to explore the ancient Greek and Roman mythology. It is expected that the research student should know the myths of Zeus, Adonis, Persephone, Aphrodite or Venus, Apollo, Diana, Hyperion, Narcissus, and Osiris. Robert Grave's *Greek Mythology* is a good introduction of the ancient myths. The other reference books are *Oxford Dictionary of Classical Terms* and *Oxford Companion of English Literature.*

(e) **Linguistics.** Philology was a compulsory paper in M.A. (English) in all Indian Universities. It was thought that a knowledge of the history of English language and its relations with other European languages was of great help to the students for an overall view of the subject of their study. But the great drawback of the system was that qualified teachers were not available. As most of the teachers did not exactly know the sound systems of English and German, they could not explain Grimm's Law to the students nor could they say how Old English *hus* was changed into Modern English *house.* The practical difficulties made the Boards of studies drop philology from the English course.

The recent developments in linguistics have made us think over the matter again. Now, philology is termed Historical Linguistics and a new branch Descriptive Linguistics has come up. Historical linguistics studies the growth and development of language in different periods. Ferdinand de Saussure rightly named it the diachromic study of language. The diachromic study of language is not possible unless a detailed study of language is made in a given period, the study which we call synchronic study of language and which is better known as Descriptive Linguistics. The following are the different aspects of descriptive linguistics :

(i) *Phonetics* studies speech sounds in general.

(ii) *Phonology* studies the sound system of a language.

(iii) *Morphology,* studies how morphemes are combined into words.

(iv) *Syntax* studies the sentence structure of language.

(v) *Semantics* studies meaning.

The findings of modern linguistics, which is largely descriptive linguistics, have revolutionised our notion of language and made us approach literature in a new way. The basic concepts are summarised.

(i) Speech is primary. Language is primarily speech. Writing system was developed much later. Even today there are many tribal languages that have no writing system. If the speakers of a modern language decide to adopt a new writing system, the language will not change.

(ii) Language is a structured system. The relationship between a word and its meaning is arbitrary. We cannot explain why we call a dog a dog. The meaning of a word is determined by its relationship to other words. A sound or word cannot have a meaning in isolation; it can be understood in relation to other sounds and words. Secondly, every language has a system of recognizing sounds and organizing the set of recognized sounds into words and words into sentences. De Saussure said that there are two aspects of language; langue and parole. Langue is the system of language and parole the actual utterances.

(iii) Meaning of grammar. Earlier it was believed that only the educated people knew grammar. Now we know that in the past people meant by grammar the formal analysis of a language. An illiterate or even a literate man was considered to be ignorant of grammar because he could not formally analyse his language. Modern linguists are of the view that there are three kinds of grammar. The first is the native speaker's grammar which helps him understand all the sentences of his language and make distinction between a sentence and a non-sentence. The second is teacher/student grammar which is meant for teaching purpose and which is largely prescriptive. The third is the linguist's grammar which describes the rules of a language.

Related to it is Chomsky's concept of competence and performance. The ideal hearer-speaker has the ability to understand and produce all the sentences of his language. Competence is related to the understanding ability and performance to producing ability.

(iv) **Deep structure and surface structure.** According to Chomsky a native speaker makes a semantic interpretation of perceived reality. That semantic interpretation is the deep structure. Through a set of rules the contents of the deep structure are transformed into the surface structure. For example the sentence *I ordered him to pay her* is a combination of two structures at the deep level *I ordered him* and the embedded sentence *He pay her.* The second sentence *I promised him to pay her* has the deep structure *I promised him* and the embedded sentence *I pay her.* At the surface level both the sentences *I ordered him to pay her* and *I promised him to pay her* have the same structure but at the deep level different structures.[4]

The findings of modern linguistics have made a tremendous impact on the methods of textual analysis. Not to go in detail, it will suffice to say that stylistics, a method of textual analysis in Britain and America, Formalism of Russia and Structuralism, Post-structuralism and Deconstruction, the most modern critical approaches to literature, are all linguistics-oriented.

(f) **Psychology.** Literature and psychology are closely related. We can say literature is an imaginative presentation of man's psyche and psychology its scientific description. Freud once said that poets and novelists had discovered the unconscious long before him; all that he did was that he gave a scientific explanation to it. Freud was modest in his remark. We know that poets, novelists and dramatists have all been influenced by his psychology. William James's concept of the consciousness made the novelists James Joyce, Virginia Woolf and Dorothy Richardson write a new kind of novel which is now known as the stream-of-consciousness novel.

What is more important is that psychology has provided a new approach to literature. Freud's interpretation of *King Lear* and Dr. Jones's of *Hamlet* are bold and original. Besides Freud's contention that a creative writer is a neurotic and minor literature a kind of day-dreaming has made critics analyse a literary text in a new way. Jung's seminal essays "Psychology and literature" and "Archetypes of the Collective Unconscious" have given birth to Archetypal or Myth Criticism.*

(g) Christianity. Old English poetry is basically religious. During the period of the renaissance and reformation there were two currents in English literature: the secular and the religious. The secular poets occasionally exposed the evils practices of the holy men and the church. The religious poets continued the old tradition. Spenser was the finest product of the renaissance and the reformation. The rise of Protestantism and the authoritative translation of the Bible into English in 1611 made a lasting effect on the English poets.

Apart from the Morality, Mystery and Miracle plays, Spenser's *Fairy Queen,* Donne's *Holy Sonnets,* Herbert's *The Temple,* Milton's *Paradise Lost* and *Paradise Regained,* Bunyan's *Pilgrim's Progress,* Christiana Rossetti's and Hopkins's poems which are essentially religious, great dramatists, poets and novelists have maintained the Christain spirit in their works. In order that we can fully appreciate the Christian point of view embedded in plays like Shakespeare's *The Tempest* or Eliot's *Murder in the Cathedral* or Shaw's *Saint Joan* we must know the history of Christianity, the Church and the teachings of the Bible.

(h) Anthropology and Sociology. Anthropology is the scientific study of man's origin, his division into different races and cultures. Sociology makes the scientific study of the

* Myth or Archetypal criticism is described in brief in methods.

development of different social groups and their interactions and structure of society. Sir James Frazer in his monumental book *the Golden Bough* propounded the theory that the development of society has been from the stage of magic through religion to science and contended that myths are the explanations of the cycle of seasons. Frazer's theory has made us look at the ancient myths, primitive rituals and old customs in a more scientific way. Now we do not look down upon myths as only stories but take them seriously because we have come to know that in our scientific age we, too, make myths. The findings of the modern anthropologists have provided a rich source of materials for the modern poets and novelists. Even serious poets like Eliot and Auden made full use of the ancient myths interpreting them as the anthropologists did.

Analyses of the social structure and group and class relations by eminent sociologists like Marx, Gramsci, Weber, MecIver and many others have made it clear that a work of art, (though it is a product of an individual and bears his stamp), always represents the ideas of his class in relation to the class which is in conflict with it. This is why in every age authors of a class in spite of their individuality share common ideas and common themes.

Armed with the elementary knowledge of these subjects, the researcher is in a better position to analyse the literary texts, understand the different critical theories and define his critical stance while writing his thesis.

REFERENCES

1. Richard D. Altick, *The Art of Literary Research* (New York : W.W. Norton Company, 1963), 16-41.
2. Irving Ribner, *William Shakespeare* (New York : John Wiley & Sons, 1969), Chapter II.
3. Paul de Man's essay "The Resistance to Theory," *Yale French Review,* 63, 1982, argues in favour of literary theory.
4. W.G. Moulton's article "Linguistics" *The Aims and Methods of Scholarship in Modern Languages and Literatures,* ed. James Thorpe, (Hyderabad : ASRC, 1970) and J.P.B. Allen's "Some Basic Concepts in Linguistics" *Papers in Applied Linguistics,* Vol. 2, ed. JPB Allen and S. Pit Corder, (London : Oxford Univ. Press, 1975) are good introductions for research students.

3

Materials and Tools of Research

What can be the materials and tools of research? A research student of literature may ask. In science, he will say, materials are the objects of nature and the tools are scientific instruments. He is right in his questionings. A scientist examines an object of nature and differentiates it from other objects by defining its properties. Likewise he observes different phenomena of nature and tries to discover the same law operating behind them, first by formulating a hypothesis and, later on, by testing it.

Can we adopt the same kind of method in literary research? Yes, we can. Literary research is equally systematic, methodical and objective, hence scientific; it has specific materials for investigation and scientific tools for arriving at a conclusion or formulating a theory. Only we have to remember that Aristotle applied the same principles in Physics, Politics and Poetics.

The materials of literary research are manuscripts and printed books. By manuscripts we mean all the works of an author whether written in his own hand-writing* or in the writings of others. Printed books and manuscripts include all the texts, letters, diaries, journals, memoirs and reviews and critical comments and criticism by the author.

In science the basic tools are observation and experiment. In literature, too, the basic tools are observation and experiment.** Of course, we do not make experiments in the

* A manuscript which is in the author's hand-writing is called a "holograph"

** By experiment is meant the scientific study of manuscripts and printed books, their paper, date and binding.

way a physicist does. In this respect we are nearer to sociology and history.

(I) MATERIALS

Manuscripts can be divided into two broad divisions: manuscripts in cursive writing before the introduction of the printing machine in England and manuscripts when the spellings were modernised in the eighteenth century and a uniformity was reached in the shape of the letters.

The problems that the Old English and Middle English manuscripts pose are the following :

(a) Old English is almost foreign even to the native English speakers.

(b) Spellings of Old English words are also strikingly different from those of New English words.

(c) There was no uniformity in the shape of the written symbols (graphemes). For example the letters *a* or *b* could be written in many ways.*

(d) Though Middle English is very near to New English, many of its words are obsolete and some of them have changed semantically.

(e) The syntax of Middle English is also different in many cases. For example, the pronouns *its* and *his* were interchangeable and two negatives made a sentence negative.

(f) The authors in most cases wanted to remain anonymous and never dated the texts.

New English manuscripts pose little problems excepting these two :

(a) A large number of manuscripts are unsigned.

(b) The writing is illegible when the writer is in a hurry or tired.

Editions. Caxton set up his printing machine in 1476. It is unnecessary here to record the books he printed and published.

---

* For details, see Chauncey Sanders, *An Introduction to Research in Literary History* (New York: Macmillan, (1963), 3-5 and plate no. 1 and 2. The plates are reproduced from R.B. McKerrow, *An Introduction to Bibliography*, (Oxford).

We have only to know that the introduction of the press was revolutionary. Uptill then a book was copied by scribes. The work was tedious, time-taking and in most cases boring. Secondly, the scribes made mistakes while copying and the result was that the manuscripts differed considerably. Now the press made the work easier and more accurate. However printed editions are not always reliable and pose before the research student or scholar the following problems :

(a) There is a considerable difference between a manuscript and a printed edition.

(b) The number of an edition or reprint is seldom printed.

(c) The year of publication is rarely recorded.

(d) Polemical articles do not bear the authors' names.

(e) There are pirated editions and forged manuscripts.

Paper. The paper of a text is also a part of the materials of research. The study of the paper is important for determining the date of a text and ascertaining its genuineness. A paper expert will tell us the age of a paper after examining its quality and watermark. Once we have come to know the date of the paper of a text we can safely assume that the text was written after the date. If a forgerer presents a manuscript claiming that it was written in the thirteenth century, we can examine its genuineness by determining the date of the paper.

Ink. Ink is the third important part of the materials. To take a simple example, if some one comes with a manuscript written with a ball-point pen and claims that it belongs to the nineteenth century, we will at once say that he is cheating us because ball-point pens did not exist at that time. A book on the history of ink will tell us kinds of ink which were used in different ages.

The complex nature and size of materials has made literary research a really difficult and also interesting form of investigation for the discovery of truth.

Finding materials. The nature of finding materials depends on the topic. If we are to edit a text, say Milton's *Paradise Lost,* we have to look for the manuscripts, the different editions, critical commentaries and relevant criticism. Suppose we are writing a doctoral dissertation on W.B. Yeats's use of myths, we need not consult the manuscripts. We have to study books on Irish mythology, the books discussing myths in general, all the works of Yeats and critical works on Yeats.

But how to know the titles of books, their authors and places of publication? The best source is, of course, *Cambridge Bibliography of Literature.* The other useful general bibliography is PMLA bibliography which is published every year. *Oxford History of English Literature, Pelican Guide to English Literature, A Literary History of America* and *A Literary History of England* contain useful bibliography. *The English Novel* and *The English Poetry* edited by A.E. Dyson contain bibliography on the more important British novelists and poets and, in addition, contain useful introduction to each of the selected authors. Nowadays critical books on authors contain selected bibliography which includes both primary and secondary sources. For more recent books the best is *Books in Print* which is published every year. The research student can find materials there in three ways : authorwise, titlewise and subjectwise.

All university libraries have adopted the decimal system of classification. It is easy to locate books where there is the open system after consulting the cards which are indexed titlewise and authorwise and which are stored in drawers in the entrance hall. Some prestigious libraries have computerised the system. The great benefit is that a reader after necessary payment can collect information about the books on the subject in these libraries. Journals are a very useful part of bibliography. Every library displays the recent arrivals on a board. For the old issues the research student should go to the reference section or the archives where journals are kept.

The libraries of national importance maintain the manuscripts of old authors. For the living authors, the best sources are the authors themselves or their trustees. In England, the manuscripts of most of the authors upto the nineteenth century are preserved in the university or public libraries. Since writing in English began in India in the last quarter of the nineteenth century (we are not concerned with books in Sanskrit, Arabic, Persian, Urdu, Hindi and the regional languages here) manuscripts can be located in the houses of the authors or their inheritors. The best way, therefore, is to contact the authors or their trustees for the study of manuscripts. In England and America, too, research students or scholars approach the authors or their trustees to consult manuscripts for copyright reasons.

(II) TOOLS OF RESEARCH

The basic tools; observation and experiment, are common to all kinds of research. Here we are concerned with the special tools of literary research, although some of them are used in natural and social sciences. The tools of literary research are :

(a) Bibliography, (b) Note System, (c) Scientific tools and (d) Textual analysis.

(a) Bibliography. The word bibliography usually means a list of books and articles on a given subject or an author. In literary research the term means "the science of books" and has a wider denotation. We may divide bibliography into four kinds.

(i) Historical bibliography, (ii) Bibliothecal bibliography, (iii) Enumerative bibliography and (iv) Practical bibliography.

(i) Historical bibliography deals with the history of book production which includes the history of writing, printing, binding, illustrating, publishing and selling. By a successful use of historical bibliography we determine the date of a text. It is a well known fact that there has been a gradual development in the process of making paper, science of printing and art of writing. The historical bibliography is equally useful in editing a text, determining its authenticity and attributing it to an author. We shall discuss its use in Chapter IV.

(ii) Bibliothecal bibliography helps us locate books and journals in a library. Primarily concerned with library science and history of library it gives an idea about the classification and location of important libraries. Nowadays all modern libraries use the decimal system of classification and arrange cards author-wise and title-wise alphabetically. The reference section is maintained separately and there is the archives where old journals and manuscripts are housed.

In modern times knowledge has fairly advanced and no subject can be studied in isolation. The research student should not confine himself to the topic of research nor limit his knowledge to the subject of specialisation but study books related to his research, though they may belong to other subjects. Some prestigious libraries prepare a list of books available on a subject but the list must not be considered final and the research student should make use of bibliothecal bibliography. Now some libraries have computerised the information system but we must know that computers cannot surpass the human brain. It is the human brain that feeds data to computers. Internet has its own limitations.

(iii) Enumerative bibliography helps the research student know the books he actually needs. The standard bibliographies, *Cambridge Bibliography of English Literature* and *MLA Bibliography* published every year help the student prepare a working bibliography. The other useful source is *Books in Print* published every year and maintained by every university library. (For details read the section Finding Materials in this very chapter).

(iv) Practical bibliography is concerned with the methods of work of student and author — reading, research, compilation of notes and bibliography, preparation of the manuscript, typing of the research paper or the thesis.

Bibliography is usually divided into two main divisions : Primary sources and secondary sources.

The Primary Sources consist of all the writings of an author — literary texts (poems, plays, novels, essays), autobiography, diary, journals, letters and memoirs. The letters, diaries, journals and reminiscences of his close friends and contemporaries are also included in the primary sources. Some scholars include standard biographies in the list of primary sources. The important point to note is that we include only those materials in the list of primary sources, which give us a first hand knowledge of the author.

The Secondary Sources include books on the works of the author. These are usually critical books, research papers notes, reviews, comments and unpublished theses.

The main difference between the two is that the primary sources are the subject of investigation and the secondary sources help us understand, analyse and interpret the primary sources. Both are important but our main concern is always the primary sources.

(b) Note system. Notes provide facts for future reference. Note taking helps students concentrate attention during lectures and study of books. Different people have different reasons for taking notes, and to a considerable extent the reason dictates the way in which the notes should be taken. There is no hard and fast rule. However, in literary research a technique has been developed for taking notes, which is generally known as note-system.

Notes can be broadly divided into two groups :

(i) Lecture Notes.

(ii) Text notes.

(i) *Lecture notes.* There are basic differences between college lectures and university lectures. First of all the university lecturer speaks much faster because he expects his students to take down only bare facts. Since he assumes more general knowledge and expects his students to spend more time in the university library, he is more selective, and unless he enlarges upon a special aspect, he will not give facts. Indeed he will refer to source material, perhaps even write the title of books and journals, names of authors and the uncommon or technical words on the blackboard. In fact he, in most cases, does not try to "teach" the post-graduate or M.Phil. or Ph.D. students* everything there is to know on the subject; instead he guides them. This means that the research student has to concentrate more and be more selective in the classroom. Usually, besides a few facts or quotations, the lecturer provides a valuable structure and references which are worth-noting.

The best way to take lecture notes is to note the main points of argument in the hall and immediately after the lecture, because the contents of the lecture are still fresh in memory, to enlarge it and compare it with the notes of the classfellows to ascertain that all the points have been taken down.

---

* In most universities, research students have to successfully complete courses before they start writing thesis or doctoral dissertation.

(ii) *Text notes*. Text notes mean notes taken from books and journals in libraries. The text notes can be divided into bibliographical notes and subject notes.

Bibliographical notes are concerned with the location of books in libraries and for use in the preparation of footnotes and bibliography. For bibliographical notes, cards (I prefer the soft cards) of 3" × 5" size should be bought and kept in card boxes. There should be an index of cards also.

The card should contain the following information :

(i) The call number.

(ii) Author and the title of the book.

(iii) Edition and Publisher.

(iv) Library.

(v) Contents.

An illustration is given how to prepare the card :

Call No.	410.9 L 9 ROB
Author, title	Robins, RH, *A Short History of Linguistics* 1979 (2nd ed., Longman, London)
Library	Kanpur University Library
Contents	Greece, Rome, Middle Ages, Renaissance, Modern Times, Comparative and Historical linguistics in the 19th century, linguistics in the present age.

Subject notes are specific and are meant to be incorporated in the main body of the thesis or dissertation. The research student notes down the matters he considers to be of importance. Like the bibliographical cards, he should have subject-note cards and boxes.

The following system is to be followed for subject notes :

(i) The card should be of 5" × 8" size.

(ii) One card should contain one idea, fact or concept.

(iii) There should be a heading at the top of each card.

(iv) There should be sufficient information to identify each note.

(v) There should be information whether the matter written on the card is a paraphrase or verbatim quotation.

(vi) The card should be labelled in sequence such as a b c and so on if the information is much.

An illustration of the subject card is given below.

Self-consciousness and English Poetry

Robert Rehder 821.7

Rehder considers modern poetry an expression of the unconscious, a poetry of self analysis.

"Modern poetry is, more than anything else, a poetry of self-analysis, of the exploration of consciousness that is, the exploration of consciousness, both its explicit and implicit subject. It is a poetry that tries to bring more and more of the life of the mind to consciousness. Thus, it becomes a poetry interested in the exploration or representation of the unconscious," p. 17.

In the subject-note there is no need to write the title of the book; it is already there in the bibliographical note. Here the heading of the chapter, author's name and the index number are sufficient. What is important is the preparation of the note; there is no need to write the title *Wordsworth and the Beginnings of Modern Poetry* nor the publisher's name nor the year of publication.

The great problem before a research student is how to take notes because he has not been trained to do it in his post-graduate course. The technique is described in brief.

The first problem that a research student faces is what ideas to note down and which ideas to ignore. In the beginning he is attracted towards only those points that seem to have direct relation to his topic. He is more interested in the conclusion than in the arguments and facts. He should know that comments that are not supported by facts, and conclusions without logical arguments do not have any value. Therefore, the research student must read the book thoroughly and during the period of his study insert slips between the pages he considers to be containing important ideas and facts and, later on, when he has finished the book, take down notes.

The second problem is when to paraphrase and when to quote verbatim. The usual practice is to summarise an argument spreading over a page or more. For shorter passages it is always better to paraphrase them. A thesis littered with quotations seems an ill-worked pastiche. Only those passages are to be quoted that cannot be easily paraphrased or that are to be analysed and discussed. In all cases —summary, paraphrase and verbatim quotation —pages must be referred to.

The third problem is how much note to be taken. It is better to take down plenty of notes. In the beginning, it is very difficult to decide which notes will be useful. Sometimes it has been found that the notes that seemed unimportant in the beginning proved to be really important.

Lastly, the style of taking notes. Should we use our own abbreviations? Since subject notes are for personal use, the researcher can use the standard abbreviations and also invent his own. The standard abbreviations are :*

app.	appendix	Ms.	manuscript
c.	circa (about), century	Mss.	manuscripts
ch.	chapter	n.d.	no date, not dated
cf.	compare	no.	number
do	ditto	op. cit.	in the work cited
ed.	editor, edited by	p., pp.	page, pages
e.g.	for example	passim	everywhere
esp.	especially	pref.	preface
et al.	and others	pseud.	pseudonym
et sq.	and the following	supp.	supplement
ff.	flourished	trans.	translation
ibid	in the same place	tr.	translator
idem	the same	viz.	namely
i.e.	that is	v., vide	see
ill.	illustration or illustrated	v. infra	see below
loc. cit.	in the place cited	v, supra	see above
lib. cat.	library catalogue	vol.	volume

* For a detailed list of abbreviations, see *Thesis and Assignment Writing* and *MLA Handbook for the writers of Research Papers.*

He can invent abbreviations like shd. for should, cd. for could, ww for WordsWorth and the like. However, he should be cautious enough not to confuse one with the other.*

(c) **Scientific tools.** Chauncey Sanders has included magnifying glass, camera, microscope and Lovibond Tintometer Glasses in the list of scientific tools.[1] A magnifying glass is needed to decipher some of the faint letters in a manuscript. For making a copy of a manuscript he advises to use a photostat machine (now it has been replaced by an electrostat machine, also known as xerox machine). If the manuscript is too delicate, a good camera fitted with a long roll of film, like a motion picture film, can be used to take the photograph of the manuscript. The entire text, now converted into a microfilm, can be read with the help of some lighting device. The colour of the ink is compared with the help of the Lovibond Tintometer Glasses. Microscopes are used in examining handwriting, especially for the purpose of detecting forgeries, in transcribing manuscripts and in discovering the composition of paper.

In India, these scientific devices can be used now as some of the Indian creative writers have stopped writing and their manuscripts need a critical or definitive edition. Since Sanders and Altick have focussed their attention mainly on biographical method, bibliography and textual criticism, they have ignored the most important method, literary criticism and Theories, which is the most common method of research adopted by research students in Indian universities. Therefore, the following tools may be added to Sander's list :

(i) *Tape recorder* : Earlier, the recording of plays and poems were made on discs of plastic. Nowadays, these are available in cassettes which are light and handy. The meaning of a poem, a story or a play is more clear when we hear its reading. Modern poets have recorded their poems and their cassettes are available. A research student can benefit immensely by them if he listens to them carefully. English, though widely popular in India, is a foreign language and very few Indians are able to catch the intonation of the language. For an Indian

* See *The Art of Literary Research*, 171-180 and *An Introduction to Research in Literary History*, 290-97.

student it is important that he should be able to understand the tone and rhythm of the poems and plays on which he is doing research, which is possible only when he listens to the cassettes repeatedly and trains his ears to the sounds of English.

(ii) *Television and VCR* : Films have been made on standard works of Literatures. If a poem is meant for reading and listening, a play is meant for staging and reading. Drama is primarily a visual art. We cannot appreciate a play fully unless we see it acted. We can read *Hamlet* independently or with the help of commentators and critics, but the real pleasure and appreciation lies in the film on *Hamlet* in which Lawrence Olivier has acted the main role.

Similarly, the life-history of important writers has also been recorded in the celluloid and happily their video cassettes are available at moderate prices. With the help of television and video cassette recorder, the research student can "see" the places where the author lived, the occasions when he wrote his poetry or novel, and the people with whom he was on intimate terms.

(d) Textual analysis. Textual analysis is the most important tool of research in literature. By textual analysis we are able to demonstrate how the different components of a literary text are related to one another and how the entire whole is dependent for its meaning on its parts and yet has a meaning independent of them.

Although many scholars and critics had noticed earlier the importance of the analysis of a poem without reference to its author and his biography, it was I.A. Richards who first demonstrated how subjectivity creeps into our interpretation of poem. He devised a method, Practical Criticism, by which we can analyse and interpret a poem objectively. He said that there are four kinds of meaning, sense, feeling, tone and intention, and in order that we should understand a poem as it is we have to take note of all the four. His followers, especially James Reeves, H. Coombes and S.H. Burton, have developed this tool to a certain precision.* Cleanth Brooks in collaboration with Robert Penn Warren made use of textual analysis in *Understanding Poetry* and *Understanding Drama* and with R. Heilman *Understanding Fiction* with such a perfection that these books are still our model.

Textual analysis is concerned with the words and syntactical structure of the text and their inter-relationship. In the category of words it analyses simile, metaphor, metonymy, irony imagery, symbolism and other figures of speech. In the second group are the metre system and stanza form, usually called versification.

A literary work of art is an imaginative reproduction of reality. The creative writer does not write about an idea, experience, feeling or emotion like an average man. His use of language is never referential; it is always emotive. The desired effect is made by means of simile, metaphor, metonymy, irony, paradox, imagery, symbolism, backgrounding and foregrounding. The sound effect is created by the use of assonance, consonance and rhyme. In poetry a particular metre and a particular stanza form are chosen for the desired expression of the experience or idea. Sometimes the poet varies the length of lines, deviates from the regularity of the metre he is using in a particular poem, and breaks away from the traditional stanza form.

A student of literature who goes for the textual analysis of a literary work must know the meaning of these literary terms.

Forms of Literature	:	Poetry, drama, novel, essay, short-story, satire, parody and allegory.
Forms of Poetry	:	Epic, mock epic, narrative poetry, ode, lyric, sonnet, ballad, elegy, pastoral and dramatic monologue.
Forms of Drama	:	Tragedy, comedy, tragi-comedy, melodrama and burlesque.

* James Reeves, *The Critical Sense,* H Coombes, *Literature and Criticism,* S.H. Burton, *The Criticism of Prose* and *The Criticism of Poetry,* Marjorie Boulton, *The Anatomy of Poetry, The Anatomy of Drama* and *The Anatomy of Novel.*

Forms of Novel	:	Historical novel, social novel, psychological novel and scientific fiction.
Literary devices	:	Alliteration (assonance and consonance) imagery, contrast and juxtaposition, irony, paradox, parallelism, foregrounding, backgrounding, repetition, motif, leit-motif, empathy, tone (overtone and undertone), metaphor, metonymy, synedoche, symbolism and refrain.
Style	:	Naturalism, realism, impressionism, magic realism, expressionism, futurism and interior monologue.

In English poetry verification has two aspects : metre system and stanza form. There are six metres in English poetry : Iambus, Trochee, Anapaest, Dactyl, Pyrrhus and Spondee of which the most common are Iambus and Trochee. The other metres are used for variation to remove the monotony of Iambus and Trochee. The length of a line is determined by the number of feet which in turn is determined by the number of stresses.

The stanza is a unit in a poem. English poets, at first, followed the Latin stanza forms in the beginning but later on made experiments and invented the stanza forms which are typically English. The most common stanza forms are :

Couplet	:	a pair of rhymed lines.
Heroic couplet	:	a pair of rhymed lines in iambic pentameter.
Tercet or Triplet	:	Three lines rhyming together, often used for humour.
Octosyllabic couplet	:	a pair of rhymed lines in tetrameter.
Terza Rima	:	a stanza of three lines with rhyme-scheme aba, bcb, cdc and so on.
Quatrain	:	a four line stanza.
Ballad Stanza	:	alternating four and three foot lines.
Heroic Quatrain	:	iambic pentameter rhyming ab, ab.
Rhyme Royal	:	a seven line iambic pentameter stanza rhyming ab, ab, b, cc.

Ottava Rima : an eight line iambic pentameter stanza rhyming ab, ab, ab, cc.

Spenserian Stanza : a nine line stanza, the first eight lines in iambic pentameter and the ninth hexameter (Alexandrine) rhyming ab, ab, bc, bc, c.

The textual analyst gives due importance to the parts but knows that their importance lies in their relation to the poem which is an organic whole. In his analysis he demonstrates how the irrelevant local texture enriches the logical structure of the poem. He will not be led astray by the beauty of an image, an expression or a line but will examine it in the total structure of the poem.

The concluding lines of Yeats's "Among School Children" give us an idea of the nature of a work of art.*

O chestnut tree, great-rooted blossomer,
Are you the leaf, the blossom or the bole?

The chestnut is all the three and yet more than that. A poem is its words, its syntactical structure, its stanza form and its argument but it is something more than its parts; it is an organic whole, the verbal icon. The textual analysis discovers and demonstrates the truth.

NOTE

1. Chauncey Sanders, *An Introduction to Research in Literary History,* 88-90.

---

* Yeats surely did not write what a poem should be. He wrote the lines in a different context and the meaning of the lines is highly philosophical but the image he has referred to serves my purpose. I do not have any intention to misinterpret the poem or the lines quoted.

4

METHODS OF RESEARCH : BIOGRAPHY, HISTORY OF IDEAS AND TECHNIQUE

In Britain, the USA, Canada, and other English speaking countries literary research is usually confined to biography and editing of texts (now generally termed Bibliographical and Textual Criticism) and a distinction between a scholar and critic is made. Naturally, the researcher in the British and American universities knows what is he going to do, why he is going to do it and how he will do it. He defines his methodology categorically and seldom deviates from his critical stance. Even when he is interpreting the facts, he adopts a particular critical approach and method of analysis.

In India, the situation is different. Biography is not considered a method of research nor is editing. The only kind of research which is most popular is the critical interpretation of an author's works.

Usually, research students mix up two or three approaches to literature, seldom aware of the fact that their method, a heterogeneous blend, makes their viewpoint vague and blurred.

In the pages that follow three main methods of literary research are described in brief. These methods are :

(a) Biography.

(b) Bibliographical and Textual Criticism.

(c) Literary Criticism.

(I) BIOGRAPHY

I.A. Richards, after reading the responses to the ten poems he had given to his undergraduate students to study, concluded that a poem should be read in its own terms and we should not take interest in the biography of the poet as it prejudices us. Wimsatt and Beardsley in their famous articles "Intentional Fallacy" and "Affective Fallacy" considered Richards subjective in approach because he took notice of the author's intention. They may be right in their effort to make criticism more objective and systematic but they forget the fact that no work of art can be completely separated from its creator; it always bears the stamp of his personality. The reader, after finishing a novel or a poem, wants to know about its author. He asks: who wrote it? What kind of man was he? Under what circumstances did he write it? Are all the events described a part of his personal experience? Do the characters depicted in it come from real life? The formalist critic remains unconcerned with these. But we want to know them and there is the biographer to help us. He tells the author's life story correlating his literary output with the important events of his life.

Biography is an important kind of research. In the past, authors maintained anonymity; the work was more important. The ancient writers wrote almost nothing about them nor did other people. Naturally, their life remained shrouded in mystery after death, giving birth to a number of fictitious stories and myths. The most common myth about the great ancient poets is their illiteracy, humble birth and blindness. Homer is reputed to be blind, Valmiki a bird-hunter, Kalidas an idiot, Shakespeare a poacher. This fictionalising of facts and covering them with a romantic aura created problems for scholars and critics. It became increasingly difficult to determine their time and date, list the works they really composed and determine their chronology. In spite of continued researches, the dates of many important writers are debatable and their life-history inauthentic.

It was only in the seventeenth century that literary biographies began to be written. Dr. Samuel Johnson wrote the biographies, of course, sketchy, of fifty-two poets, in his monumental work *The Lives of the Poets.* Sir John Hawkins, who had been in the company of Johnson, wrote *Life* (1787) of the great personality. But the real writing of biography began with Boswell's *Johnson*, which is still read with great interest and the Johnson we know today is Boswell's Johnson.

Since Boswell's *Johnson,* biography has developed on different lines. We have bio-critical biographies like A.N. Jeffares's *W.B. Yeats* : *Man and the Poet,* Donald Sheaffers *Eugene O'Neill: Son and Artist,* Mckenzie's *Charles Dickens* and *Haight's George Eliot.* In the second category are biographies focussing on the milieu of the author, of which Edmund Malone's *Life of Dryden* (1800) and David Mason's *Life of Milton* (1859-80) are the most famous. In the third category are the biographies which narrate the life-story of a writer from ethical or moral point of view. Edward Dowden's *Shakespeare* and *Shelley* are the representative examples. The fourth category of biographies is that of psychological biography in which the biographer is more concerned with the exploration and presentation of the writer's inner working of mind. Lytton Strachey's *Eminent Victorians* is a psychological biography. The twentieth century biographers have made the art of biography objective and exact. The following are the characteristics of the modern biography :

(i) It shows the author's growth of mind. Modern biographers are more interested in presenting the inner development of the authors. All the external events and influences are studied in relation to the shaping of an author's thought and art. Herbert Read's *Wordsworth* and Ricardo Quintana's *Swift* are more concerned with the growth of the mind of these authors than with the presentation of the main events in their life.

(ii) It tells us more accurately about the author's time and people. An author is a product of his time and he can be best understood and evaluated if we place him among the people with whom he had lived. Ribner's biography of Shakespeare bears the title *William Shakespeare* : *An Introduction to His Life, Times and Theatre* and describes in brief the English renaissance, life in England in the Elizabethan period, the drama before Shakespeare, Elizabethan theatres, a list of publication of Shakespeare's plays, Shakespeare's criticism and the staging of Shakespeare's plays upto the present time.

(iii) It explains some of the obscure passages in the author's work. Usually, an author makes use of his personal experiences in his work. Sometimes a talk in a party, a joke made by a friend or a private experience are alluded. A good biography narrates the event, or the joke or the experience and relates it to the allusion made in the work. J. Hone's biography of W.B. Yeats explains many of the obscure passages in his plays and poems. Donald Sheaffer's biography tells us that O'Neill was fond of startling and unusual titles for his plays. *Mourning Becomes Electra* bears an unusual title and Sheaffer describes how O'Neill invented it and deliberately made it ambiguous to mean both "It befits Electra to mourn" and "Mourning (clothes) befit Electra."

(iv) It explodes some of the myths about an author. It is usual for the admirers to create myths about their favourite author. There are a number of anecdotes ascribed to George Bernard Shaw, but now we all know that a large number of them are mere inventions. Similarly E.E. Cummings, since he had made bold experiments in poetic forms and language, was considered to be highly modern in his personal life. Now, we all know, thanks to his biographers, that he was traditional in his personal life and behaviour and he never allowed an electrical lamp in his house!

Now that the art of biography has become more systematic and objective, an important research activity, the goals of a literary biographer can be enumerated as follows :

(i) Disinterested study of the author's life and ideas,

(ii) situational correlation between the literary work and life,

(iii) distinction between fact and fiction,

(iv) avoidance of unnecessary details to make the biography interesting and project the author's personality and

(v) maintenance of an independent point of view to analyse both the positive and negative aspects of the author.

These goals determine the task of the biographer. He like a historian, collects materials from different sources : the author's autobiography, his autobiographical statements, statements and reminiscences of his friends and other acquaintances, and articles in magazines and personal interviews.

After collection of the materials which are immensely large, he marshalls them and arranges them as far as practicable in the chronological order. In order that he can correlate the events and the literary works, he must study all the works of the author and relevant criticism on them. The next task is to present the author in both light and shade without any prejudice. For this he must not hide any unpleasant truth nor twist any fact to malign the author or exonerate him from any charge levelled against. Lastly the presentation should be clear and interesting which is possible only when the biographer avoids unnecessary details and portrays the author as man and artist.

Sources and Methods of Biography

As said earlier, writing biography in modern times is a research activity and the responsibility of the biographer, like that of a scientist, is to collect all the available data for the interpretation of an author's personality.

The biographer can collect data from different sources which can be broadly divided into four categories :

(a) Data contained in official records.

(b) Information contained in semi-official reports.

(c) Statements occurring in the statements or writings of the author's circle.

(d) Material derived from the author's statement.

(a) Official records. By official records is meant records kept in school, college, public record office and the church. In Christian countries, (England was primarily a Christian country till the end of the first half of the twentieth century) the child is christened in a church. The clergyman keeps a register and enters its name and parents' name. He also performs the marriage rituals and keeps a record of the marriages of his parishioners. It is through the church records only that the date of birth, christian name, date of marriage, wife's name and family can be authentically known. The records of the church are more important for the writers who wrote under a pseudonym.

After the establishment of the universities of Oxford and Cambridge the records of colleges gained prominence but the importance of school records were never negated nor are even today. It is the school records that tell us many things about

Shakespeare that he was educated in The Stratford Grammar School where Thomas Jenkins, a graduate from St. John's College, Oxford and M.A. from Oxford University, was his teacher. We also know authentically that he served as a teacher for some time before leaving Stratford for London. For dramatists like John Lyly, George Peele, Robert Greene, Thomas Lodge and Christopher Marlowe and poets like John Donne, George Herbert and John Milton the school and college records are of immense help.

Public record offices tell us about the genealogy, inherited property and legacy of the authors. The knowledge of their family line and landed property gives us an idea or confirmation of their upbringing.

(b) Semi-official reports. Semi-official reports contain the family genealogy, family diary and family accounts book. In India people do not keep records for the reason that they are usually eaten by termites and moths and, therefore, maintain the oral tradition. England being a cold country, people maintain written records which are seldom destroyed by insects. Even in the fifteenth century people kept a record of their family line. The members of the middle-class and the upper class paid more attention to it to show that they had an ancient family line. The way an author lived can be described by the study of the family diary and family accounts book. Henslow's *Diary* is a great source of biographical information.

(c) Statements and writings of the author's circle. This kind of source is important for two reasons. The first that the author's class-fellows and friends and teachers tell us many things which the author never noticed. An author, like other human beings, maintains two kinds of relationships, formal and informal. The formal relationship is with his teachers, elders and the people with whom he has had chance contacts. These people form an opinion about him, which may be superficial or sound. However, the teachers who know him personally and have helped on some occasions can better tell about him. The school and college friends with whom he or she has been on intimate terms give us a more detailed knowledge about him or her.

During the period of his or her apprenticeship or gaining

some maturity in literary craft an author usually becomes a member of a literary circle and develops intimacy with men of letters. The statements of these literary people are of immense value. The statements can be found in the correspondences between two friends who are intimate with the author, in their diaries, in their autobiographies and in their articles in different magazines and journals.

(d) The author's statement. The author's statement about him can be found exhaustively in his autobiography, if he or she has written it, and largely in memoirs, journals and letters. The ancient writers did not write autobiography nor maintained journals but occasionally referred to their works in their writings. The moderns, helped by the press, write much about themselves. For modern writers the biographer has not to run from pillar to post in search of materials but ancient writers demand greater labour and tenacity.

Steps

The research student who chooses to write the biography of an author should take the following steps :

(a) Study of the available literary texts and relevant criticism of the author, and autobiography and biography/biographies if available.

(b) Collection of material published and unpublished in the form of letters, journals, memoirs, official records and semi-official reports.

(c) Study and critical analysis of the collected material. This stage is very important and here the biographer must be a thorough going sceptic. In order to avoid the pitfalls he/she should take notice of the following :

(i) The author's memory is not always reliable.

(ii) He/she may try to create a myth about him or her.

(iii) His or her view about others may be prejudiced in certain cases.

(iv) Members of his/her literary circle may be prejudiced and can either exaggerate the author's good qualities or be unusually harsh and sometimes invent malicious lies.

In order that the biography should be objective and impartial, the research student has to compare different kinds of statements and arrive at the conclusion after systematic investigation.*

(d) Writing. Finally, the research student has to arrange the material chronologically, delete the unnecessary details, project the author's personality with a point of view correlating the different influences on him and his literary output.

Biographical method is an art. The biographer, like a poet, has to learn his/her trade and this he/she can do by reading the standard biographies intensively.**

(II) HISTORY OF IDEAS AND TECHNIQUE

There is no need saying that every literary work has two aspects: form and content. The creative writer takes the raw material, people and events, and imposes a form — poetry, drama, novel or short story — on it. Besides, he or she organises the created work in a special way, which is his or her technique. The organized content is not meaningless; it has a meaning, an idea or a cluster of ideas. Shelley's *Prometheus Unbound* is certainly the story of Prometheus' freedom but this freedom is not of a titan but of the entire humanity. Beyond this, it is a verse drama based upon the idea of equality, liberty and fraternity of the French Revolution. Similarly *The Scarlet Letter* is a novel that deals with the hypocrisy of puritanism in New England.

Every writer has a theme or central idea in his or her literary work. The ideas are sometimes overt and at other times covert. Shakespeare's history plays are stories of the English Kings no doubt; but they also indirectly express Shakespeare's imaginative interpretation of history. Jane Austen's novels are about love and marriage. But to understand her point of view we have to study the points of view of Defoe, Fielding, Richardson and Fanny Burney.

Most of the researches being done in India are of this type; researchers trace the dominant and subsidiary ideas of

* For the mistakes of authors and biographers, see Richard D. Altick, *The Art of Literary Research*, 14-46.

** The series *The Writer and his world* will be a good beginning as a reading material.

creative writers by analyzing their literary works and other writings.

There is a difference between literature and other modes of writing such as philosophy, history, economics, psychology and sociology. A philosopher, economist, psychologist or historian collects facts and interprets them from his or her point of view. But a creative writer never does so. The ideas are there but they are all part of the human drama. Dickens's *Hard Times* is certainly a criticism of utilitarianism but it is different from Ruskin's *Unto This Last*. So is the case of *Man and Superman*; the life force theory is not discussed in the way it is done in Bergson's writings or the Preface to the play.

Professor Lovejoy suggests four broad areas of knowledge for the researchers to investigate :

"1. The influence of classical on modern thought, and of European traditions and writings on ... literature....

2. The influence of philosophical ideas on literature, ... including the impact of pervasive general conceptions upon standards of taste and morality and educational theories and methods.

3. The influence of scientific discoveries and theories in the same provinces of thought and in philosophy; the cultural effects of science.

4. The history of the development and the effects of individual, pervasive, and widely ramifying ideas or doctrines, such as evolution, progress primitivism, diverse theories of human motivation and appraisals of human nature, mechanistic and organismic conceptions of nature and society, metaphysical and historical determinism, individualism and collectivism, nationalism and racism."[1]

We may add internationalism and globalisation to the list.

Milton's *Pradise Lost* is based on the concept of the universe before Copernicus. Professor Denis Saurat has very well described Milton's universe in *Paradise Lose* in his book *Milton*. The reference to the Italian scientist Galileo looking through his telescope to examine the spots in the moon indicates that Milton was aware of the developments in modern science.

Professor L.C. Knights's *Drama and Society in the Age of Jonson* is a serious study of social history and its impact on Jacobean literature.

For this kind of research students are advised to read seriously the first two chapters titled "The Background 'The Social Scene" and "The Literary Scene" of the eight volumes of *New Pelican Guide to English Literature,* Basil Willey's *The Seventeenth Century Background, The Eighteenth Century Background, The Nineteenth Century Studies* and *More Nineteenth Century Studies*. The other indispensable book is G.M. Trevelyan's *England: A Social History*. Q.D. Leavis's *Culture and the Reading Public* and Raymond Williams' *Drama From Ibsen to Brecht* give us a good idea of the relationship between culture and literature. A new theory of literature — cultural materialism — has sprung up from Raymond Williams's critical writings.

Since in our age many developments have taken place and politics, philosophy, economics, linguistics, psychology, anthropology, sociology and history have become highly specialized branches of knowledge and have influenced both creative writers and literary critics, we shall study the new methods of research and interpretation of ideas in Chapter VII titled "Modern Criticism and Theory."

Technique

By technique we mean the method of organizing the material collected. Every writer has his or her own way of organizing or structuring the material he or she has collected. But the method of organization is neither erratic nor entirely original; it is a part of tradition. The different genres have slowly developed. The short-story is a development of the folk-tale. The novel is a development of the romance. A great writer follows tradition no doubt, but he or she makes certain innovations. Shakespeare deviated from the Italian tradition in his sonnets. He also did not follow the classical principle of the three unities.

Technique includes narration, plot-construction, characterization, symbolism and imagery in the case of a novel or a play. Modern writers have made use of impressionism, expressionism, magic realism and surrealism in their novels and plays. The interior monologue is another important method. Maximum experiments have been made in poetry. Apart from its different genres, experiments have been made in stanza and metre forms and literary tropes.

Studies like Caroline Spurgeon's *Shakespeare's Imagery and What It Tells us,* G. Wilson Knight's *The Wheel of Fire,* William Empson's *The Structure of Complex Words,* Mary Lascelles's *Jane Austen and Her Art* are studies in technique.

The researcher can do research on an author's art of characterization, plot construction, style, use of symbols and imagery, narrative technique, irony and poetic diction. But he or she should know that research on these is not an easy task. It may be that a particular character is a mythical or historical or literary figure. The researcher must make a comparison between the first characters (real or literary or mythical) and the characters under study. For example, Shakespeare took many characters from Plutarch's *Lives* in his Roman plays. While doing research, the researcher must read Plutarch's *Lives* and books on the history of Rome to discuss how far Shakespeare deviated from the prototype and how far he was successful in doing so. Similarly, while doing research on Jane Austen's art of plot-construction, the researcher must study the method of plot construction from Defoe to Fanny Burney.

For Ph.D. the researcher need not always confine himself/herself to an individual writer; he or she may study a detail of technique throughout its history, or, within a given period. The study of poetic drama in the first half of the twentieth century can be done by a student. Similarly researches can be done on the technique of the Post-Absurd drama or Post-Modernism.

A new method developed by Curtis Bradford and Jon Stallworthy is to study the different drafts of a text and by comparing them, show how the final draft was reached. The deletion of words and phrases and their replacement by other words and phrases gives us a good idea of an author's technique. The editing of a variorum is a kind of higher research.

The advice of Chauncey Sanders on the study of technique

is very practical. Pages 237 and 238 are quoted in full from his book *An Introduction to Research in Literary History*.

> The procedure to be followed in a study of technique will, of course, depend upon the type of study involved. If it is to be a study of the technique of an individual, one will turn first to similar studies of other writers. Thus he will learn what characteristics are to be considered. He must discover for each of these characteristics what might be called the norm for the kind of writing that his author practised and for the period in which his author lived. Then he will be able to determine the extent to which his author deviated from the norm. In a study of versification, for example, one would consider the forms and meters used, the proportion of feminine endings and of run-on lines, the number and nature of figures of speech, and so on. For a writer of fiction, there must be an analysis of practices in plot-construction, in setting, and in characterization. In the field of characterization, the characters may be studied in the light of their function or their importance in the story, their sex, their social status, their vocations; the author's method of treatment of his characters must also be considered — whether his characterization is achieved by means of direct exposition, through what the character does or what is said about him by other characters, or by some combination of these methods.
>
> In studying an author's technique, one should not overlook the element of creative power or genius. Great literature is not produced merely by the application of an acquired technique to borrowed material. It has already been pointed out[2] that the difference between a passage in Shakespeare's *Antony and Cleopatra* and the counterpart of that passage in North's translation of Plutarch cannot be wholly explained by saying that the former represents the application of the poetic — or dramatic — technique to the latter. And yet it may be that the study of Shakespeare's technique — the attempt to learn how some of Sir Thomas North's prose became some of the poetry of *Antony and Cleopatra*—

will not only lead to a fuller appreciation of Shakespeare's drama, but may even enable another writer to perform a similar miracle of transmutation.

There is great danger that one who chooses to study a detail of technique may lose consciousness of the fact that it belongs to the work of which it is a part. Falstaff is unquestionably linked with the *miles gloriosus* tradition, and it may be very interesting and worthwhile to study him as a part of that tradition; but he is, at the same time and perhaps even more importantly, an integral, an essential part of the Henry IV plays and of *The Merry Wives of Windsor*. The student should not allow himself to forget that taking a character or any other detail out of a work for study is likely to change the significance of the part and that of the whole. Keeping that fact always in mind, the student may safely proceed with his dissection.

If one should attempt a study of a previously unexplored *genre*, an original analysis would have to be worked out; it would be much wiser for the graduate student to choose a subject that will permit him to use a model — a good study of a similar problem — as a guide. One word of warning in this connection may not be amiss. The fact that a number of works have an element — or several elements — in common does not, *ipso facto*, unite them in a *genre*. There would be little point in studying collectively poems about bluebirds or barefoot boys, or novels involving a damsel in distress, a disguised aristocrat, and a witty peasant. To constitute a *genre*, works must have in common elements of literary significance, elements that tend to shape and give character to the finished work. The *genre* will almost certainly determine whether the work be long or short, in prose or in verse. A poem of twelve or sixteen lines, or one without rhyme, is not a sonnet; a long poem may be labeled by its author, or by publisher or by critics, "A novel in verse"; but it is not a novel. The *genre* may also specify the mood, the style, and — to some extent — the subject matter. The seventeenth-century *character* is a short piece of prose, generally in a light vein, describing a type of person more or less familiar to the reader — a man about town, a retired sea captain, a coquette, a country squire. A "Character of a Babylonian Warrior" or a "Character of the Emperor of China" would have been an anomaly.

All students of technique should keep constantly in mind the fact that technique is not the most important element in literary art. To know how to write is worth little unless one has something to say. The value of studies in technique lies in the contribution they can make to a fuller understanding on the part of the reader and the help they can give to the potential author.

NOTES

1. Quoted by Chauncey Sanders, *An Introduction to Research in Literary History*, 242.
2. *Ibid.*, 165.

5

METHODS OF RESEARCH : BIBLIOGRAPHY AND TEXTUAL CRITICISM

According to Professor Fredson Bowers "The determination of the physical, external form of a book in terms of the technical analysis of its production is the function of analytical bibliography. The application to external form identifies the discipline of descriptive bibliography. The application to internal form, or contents, is the concern of textual bibliography. Through this subdivision of its pure form, analytical bibliography thus becomes a partner in the process of textual criticism."[1]

The purpose of citing this quotation is to discuss in brief the meaning of bibliography and textual criticism and their interdependence. Bibliography has come up recently. The great editors A.W. Pollard and J. Dover Wilson, while editing texts and determining their authorship and chronology, relied solely on the words printed or written on the texts, ignoring the external form. It was much later that Dover Wilson realised the value of bibliography which is concerned with the materials that form the text. Bibliography nowadays is concerned with the art of book production, history of writing, printing, binding, illustrating, and publishing. Modern scholars now have extended it to every kind of evidence that has relation to an author or his work. Helen Gardner's "Dean Donne's Monument in St Paul's", Maynard Mack's "Pope's copy of Chaucer" and John Riley and W.K. Wimsatt's "A Supplement to *The Portraits of Alexander Pope* are all bibliographical studies.[2] Textual criticism is concerned with the structure of the text, how its different parts — Acts, scenes, speeches, sentences and words

— are related and how they form a coherent whole and express the author's intention.

Bibliography and textual criticism combined together, and it is unwise to separate them, establish the authentic text and help the literary critic analyse and interpret it better. If there is a clash between the scholar and the literary critic, we have to rely on the scholar because his method is impersonal, objective and systematic whereas that of the critic is subjective and selective. The critic bases his arguments on the text which is available to him. If it is proved that the text he has analysed contains errors, all his arguments will fall flat.

Bibliography and textual criticism precede literary history and criticism. In fact, they form the very foundation on which the edifice of literary history and criticism is built.

Editing, chronology, authenticity, attribution and source influence are the main aspects of bibliography and textual criticism.

Editing. There are good editions and there are bad editions, there are editions for children and there are editions for adults. How do we know which edition is the reliable one? Let us compare a Shakespeare play edited by A.W. Verity with the same play edited by J. Dower Wilson. We will see that both the plays bearing the same title and the same author differ largely. Which edition is more reliable? An introductory knowledge of editing will enable us to know the difference between a good edition and a bad edition, and an edition for children and an edition for adults. But for a research student, this is not sufficient; he must know the job of an editor fully in order that he should be in a position to confidently declare a text authentic and reliable.

We can divide editions into four main groups :

(a) Edition for children.

(b) Edition for adults.

(c) Critical edition/definitive edition.

(d) Variorum edition.

An edition for children differs considerably from the edition for adults. Usually, it is shorter than the original, some of the passages are either deleted entirely or reduced to smaller size.

The main reason for deletion or curtailment is the notion that the passages are beyond the comprehension of the children, The second reason is that educationists feel that certain references or descriptions shall put the teacher to embarrassment if children want them to be explained. A.W. Verity's editions of Shakespeare's plays are meant for school children. Naturally certain passages and lines are deleted to make them teachable. The other important feature of this kind of edition is substitution of archaic and uncommon words by modern and more common words. Occasionally, the syntax is simplified so that children can read the book without much difficulty.

An edition for adults is a reproduction of the original, unabridged and unexpurged. But this kind of edition cannot be relied upon for critical analysis. The literary critic must have a copy of the text that best expresses the author's intention. Intention can be defined in two ways: first, it means the feelings, emotions and ideas the author wanted to express through his work and the second, the intention the text reveals. Here, we are concerned with the second meaning, intention realised in the text. The edition for adults which is meant for general readers cannot be always a reliable text for critical analysis. We do not know how far it follows the original, if it is not a reprint of a critical edition, and how many errors have crept in when it was being composited.*

The definitive or critical edition is the only edition on which scholars and literary critics rely. It is, in fact, a product of real research. The definitive edition should :

(i) Be a correct text.

(ii) List all the sources of the text.

(iii) Explain the reason for certain departures from other editions.

---

* For detailed information on printing errors leading even eminent critics to wrong interpretation, see F. Bowers, "Textual Criticism," *Aims and Methods of Literary Scholarship*, ed. James Thorpe; Richard D. Altick, *The Art of Literary Research*; Chauncey Sanders *An Introduction to Research in Literary History*; and Bruce Harkness, "Bibliography and the Novelistic Fallacy," *Twentieth Century Criticism*, ed., Handy and Westbrook.

(iv) Place the position of the text among the complete work.

(v) Explain the allusions and gloss the words used in a special sense.

(vi) Comment on social and literary backgrounds.

(vii) Introduce the text critically.

The Arden edition of Shakespeare's plays is an example of the critical edition. The Clarendon Press, Oxford, has published a large number of complete works of the Elizabethan, Jacobean, Restoration, Eighteenth century and nineteenth century authors.

The job of an editor. The job of an editor is serious, painstaking and full of responsibility. The research student who wants to edit a text should know that his work is not like that of many Indian editors who blindly follow a printed edition of an author, write an introduction, and answer a few questions that were asked in the previous university examinations. It is expected of him that he will

(i) Produce a standard text.

(ii) Record all the previous texts.

(iii) Transcribe the manuscripts/holograph.

(iv) Collate the different texts.

(v) Emend where he thinks it necessary.

(vi) Interpret the difficult or obscure expressions and add notes to allusions.

Method of editing. When an editor decides to edit the works of an author, he faces two kinds of situation: first, the author has never been published and second, the author has been published. In the first situation the editor has to consult the manuscripts or holograph only but in the second he has to consult printed edition(s) in addition to the manuscripts/or holograph. If the author belongs to the nineteenth century or earlier periods, he faces many more additional problems. In order to prepare a standard text he has to follow the scientific method of editing.

(a) ***Collection of materials :*** The editor cannot rely on only one text; he must study all the manuscripts and printed editions which are classified as under :

(i) *Holograph,* manuscript(s) written in the handwriting of the author. Earlier the word autograph was used but since the word is being used to mean the signature of a person, the more accurate term holograph was coined.

(ii) *Manuscripts not in the author's hand but containing evidence of authorised correction.*

Sometimes authors wrote their work hurriedly and then called a scribe to write it in fair hand. Errors crept in the scribe's copy for three reasons. First, the scribe misread some of the words, second, he because of carelessness mis-spelt certain words or wrote a word that did not exist in the holograph, third, he sometimes dropped a line and, lastly, the holograph contained errors and the scribe, out of ignorance or fatigue did not correct them while copying it.

The conscientious authors usually read the fair copy and made necessary corrections. This kind of manuscript is as good as the holograph.

(iii) *Manuscripts derived from an authentic text no longer extant* : This is a common feature of the Elizabethan and Jacobean texts. In those days authors, especially the playwrights who were busy with the stage, had little time to write three or four copies and naturally asked the scribes to copy their texts. In the process the original text was lost.

(iv) *Editions supervised by the author* : After the introduction of the printing machine, the ambitious writers and enterprising publishers began to sell books to the reading public. In the later half of the seventeenth century periodicals emerged to enlarge the number of the readers. The manuscripts now were not to be copied by the scribes but were to be printed in the press. The authors began to supervise the printing of their books. Sometimes, they wrote in the Preface that they had supervised the printing and occasionally appended a list of errors corrected, usually called *errata.*

(v) *Authorised editions* : These are the editions that have received the author's approval but are not corrected by him personally.

(vi) *Posthumous editions* that were corrected or revised by the author before his death.

All these are reliable texts and the editor may choose any one of these as his copy text. Besides these, there is another kind of edition which is not always reliable and which we call unauthorised editions.

(b) ***Copy-Text :*** After collection of materials, the next step is the selection of the copy-text By the copy-text we mean the text which we consider relatively free from errors and which represents the author's intention. In the words of Fredson Bowers :

> The final purpose of the examination of the evidence of the documentary forms in which a text has been preserved is the selection of a copy-text, that is, some single form of the text on which an edition should most logically be based, and the determination of any need to synthesize this copy-text with readings from any other authoritative form. Naturally, the copy-text form must be the one which possesses the greatest original authority in the sense that it is closest to the author's lost manuscript, or is the manuscript itself.[3]

However, the matter is not that simple and we cannot always faithfully adhere to a holograph or a corrected manuscript. Chauncey Sanders has suggested methods how to select a copy-text.

(i) *Choice between the holograph and the printed text.*

In general we accept the holograph as our copy-text but in certain cases we find that the printed text is more reliable.

First, the printed text, which is based upon the manuscript in question, may contain corrections or revisions made by the author in the course of the reading the proof.

Secondly, the printed text may be based upon a later manuscript which is lost or at least not known to be extant.

Thirdly, the printed text may be a reprint of an earlier edition which is based upon a corrected manuscript now lost or not known to be extant and the manuscript in question is the earliest one.

(ii) *A holograph or any demonstratively authoritative manuscript would be preferred to the printed text in the following cases :*

First, when the printed text is unauthorised and differs materially from the manuscript.

Secondly, if the printed text is based upon a version earlier than that represented by the manuscript.

Thirdly, when the printed text is a careless and corrupt printing of the manuscript, even though it was published under the supervision of the author, the manuscript is to be preferred. Here, we have to be certain that the manuscript is both clear and consistent in expression and the printed text is inconsistent or incomprehensible.

Lastly, the manuscript is preferred if the printed text is toned down from fear of censorship or changed in some way so that it does not represent the author's real intention.

(iii) *Choice among editions.*

Sometimes no manuscript is extant but there are many editions. Now the problem is, which edition to choose as the copy-text? The general tendency is to choose the first edition or princeps. The collation of the variants of Hawthorne's *Scarlet Letter* revealed that the second edition departed from the first edition in 11 words, the third of 1850 in 37 words, fourth 1875 in 37, the fifth of 1877 in 39, the sixth of 1883 in 62 and the seventh of 1900 in 59. Because of the variants and creeping in of errors, the editor uses the method of collation for the selection of the copy-text and emendation for the establishment of the standard text.

(c) ***Collation*** **:** Collation literally means comparison of two texts in all details. In literary research the number is not limited to two texts but to all the available texts. The following steps are to be taken if the authoritative manuscript or holograph is available :

(i) Transcription of the holograph or the manuscript in fair hand.

(ii) Collection of all the editions in the author's lifetime.

(iii) Comparison of all the texts letter-by-letter, mark-by-mark and word-by-word.

(iv) Entry of the variants on the margin of the transcribed holograph which is the copy text. When the manuscript or holograph is not available, or is superseded by the printed text the following procedure is adopted.

(i) For short poems, the editor may write the lines

(stanza-wise) of different editions on a sheet of paper and number them as a b c along with the years.

(ii) For longer works, he should have a copy of the edition and prepare a working copy. He should note down all the variants in red pencil on the margin.

(iii) After considering all the versions — all those in which the author may have intervened — and collating them it is possible to decide which of them is to be chosen as the copy or basic text.

When the copy text has been finally selected, the problem arises :

(i) How closely must the new edition adhere to the copy/basic text?

(ii) When may the editor depart from his copy/basic text without making note?

(iii) When may he introduce a reading in the basic text, provided he gives the reading of the basic text in a footnote?

In other words, there are two fundamental problems :

(i) Policy to be followed in reproducing the typography of the original edition.

(ii) Policy to be followed in emending the text.

For the first problem, whether texts should be edited in accord with their contemporary spelling or in modernised form, now the general opinion is that the older texts for popular reading should be modernised. But the critical edition which is meant for scholarly use should be in the old-spelling.

The second, and more important, problem leads to emendation.

(d) ***Emendation*** : After the selection of the copy-text and collation with other texts, the final shape of the definitive edition is given through emendation with notes.

Silent alteration is done in the following situations :

(i) Turned letters.

(ii) Letters of the wrong font.

(iii) Two joined words when they do not make a new word.

(iv) Obvious mistakes in punctuation, like omission of a full-stop or note of interrogation.

Alteration with notes is a difficult task because the editor has to explain why he has done so and how the emendation makes the reading consistent with the author's style or real intention. He emends giving reasons for so doing in the following situations.

(i) *Positive errors*. If the editor finds that a particular word does not fit into the meaning of a line or sentence he can make corrections. The earlier texts of Hamlet had the word "solid" in "O that this too solid flesh would melt". Dover Wilson after the study of the manuscript and the folio corrected it to "sullied" which gives a better and more sensible meaning to the line.

(ii) *Resolution of the ambiguity* : If a sentence becomes ambiguous because of the unwanted punctuation marks, it should be made univocal by removing the punctuation marks.

(iii) *Uniformity of texture* : The same spelling should be maintained throughout the text. For example, there is an alternation between the spellings *Mustapha* and *Mustafa* in Dryden's *Don Sebastian*. The alternation of the spellings is due to the engagement of two compositors who followed two spellings. The editor should adopt only one of the two spellings to maintain uniformity.

When the main body of the text is finalised after collation and emendation, the editor has to write the Textual Introduction that should concern itself with the publishing history of the text, textual problems, reasons for the modernised form if used at all and sample Bibliographical problems, and add textual notes to explain the obsolete, archaic and obscure expressions.

The editor's contribution to our understanding of literature is fourfold. In the first place, an authoritative text reveals the author's intentions, purged of all the errors that crept into a book after he ceased to control it. Secondly, the editor through his Textual Introduction makes our knowledge of the text history richer. Thirdly, the variorum edition gives us the idea of the text in its different editions. Lastly, the editing of a text from its first to the final draft* helps understand it better and also trace the development of the author's thought and artistic perfection.

Editing is the core of literary research. Altick has rightly commented :

Textual criticism is not a labour to be undertaken lightly. It is among the most damanding of all branches of literary scholarship. The technical knowledge, the infinite patience and the reasoning powers which the ideal editor brings to his task are found combined in few men and women.[4]

(II) AUTHENTICITY AND ATTRIBUTION

When we read a book of unknown authorship we want to know the man behind it. We also want to know how many books he has written. It is easy to answer if the author is our contemporary but really difficult to do so if he was born a hundred years ago. Nowadays authors are ready to admit that they have written this book or that but it was not during the period before the renaissance because in those days the poem was more important than the poet and the concealment of authorship was encouraged. We are still not certain who wrote *Sir Gawayne and the Grene Knight* and *Beowulf and Cynewulf.* In the Tudor period the creator became more important than the creation but gentlemen usually concealed their names. They did not get their works printed and circulated their manuscripts in a limited circle. In the eighteenth century the authors got their names printed in their books but because it was an age of great political controversy and literary polemics, the authors occasionally concealed their names when they wrote heated articles or venomous satires.

Even in the nineteenth century some writers wrote under pseudonyms. Some of the novels of Jane Austen were wrongly ascribed to other authors and one to Sir Walter Scott. Since in those days novel writing was not considered worthy of women, women writers wrote under pseudonym. The Bronte sisters and Mary Evans had the pseudonym Bell brothers and George Eliot respectively. Sometimes reputed authors wrote potboilers

* See Curtis Bradford, *Yeats At Work* and Jon Stallworthy, *Between the Lines,* both published by Oxford University Press.

under pseudonym. The Oxford mathematician* concealed his name and got his famous *Alice in Wonderland* and *Through the Looking Glass* published under the pseudonym Lewis Carroll because he felt that it was not worthy of him to write a fairy-tale. Many of the articles and reviews published in the *Times Literary Supplement* were written by famous poets like T.S. Eliot, W.H. Auden, Robert Graves and C. Day Lewis but they wanted to remain anonymous. Cecil Day Lewis wrote detective novels under the pseudonym Nicholas Blake.

The large number of literary works written by anonymous writers or writers with pseudonym pose before us the problem: who wrote them? This leads us to the second question: Is the present list of books and articles ascribed to an author final and authentic?

The research that tries to solve the problem of authorship has, according to Altick, three main objectives :

(i) to identify the author of the anonymous or pseudonymous work or works attributed to wrong writers,

(ii) to decide which part(s) of a work written by two or more authors belong to whom,

(iii) to remove from the received list of a writer's works whatever pieces are not his, thereby purifying his canon.

Authenticity and attribution are two different terms. Attribution is limited to solving the problem, who wrote the work. Authenticity has a wider scope. It is concerned with the genuineness of the author, his time, date, circumstances and purpose of writing. It also examines the genuineness of a manuscript in terms of its paper, ink and writing. Since authenticity and attribution both solve the problem of authorship together, we shall consider them as the two facets of the same coin and really it will be unwise of us to separate them.

There are three ways of verifying authenticity and attribution : (a) Bibliographical, (b) External and (c) Internal. We shall discuss them briefly.

(a) Bibliographical. Bibliographical evidence saves us from forgerers. Chauncey Sanders has pointed out that M. Chasle, a

* Charles Lutwidge Dodgson.

noted French mathematician, paid 140,000 francs to an adventurer named Vrain-Lucas for hundreds of letters from various worthy personages belonging to the pre-Christian period. The credulous mathematician, later on, was told that they were forged letters all written in modern French on nineteenth century note paper. The famous forgerer William Henry Ireland (1777-1835) deceived Boswell by presenting him a Shakespearean play Vortigem. Boswell because he did not know how to verify authenticity was taken in by the forgerer. Now we know better and determine the authenticity of a text on the basis of certain evidences.

The first bibliographical evidence is the author's hand-writing. We generally take it for granted that a text written in the author's own handwriting is authentic and is his work. But this is not always applicable to the texts of the fourteenth century and of the earlier periods. It may be that the author copied a book for his personal reading.

The second evidence is the ink used or the substitute for ink. It is a well known fact that ink after a long time fades and turns brown. A forgerer cannot escape the sharp eyes of a research scholar if he uses modern ink.

The third evidence is the paper of the text. The quality of the paper and its water mark tell us about its date. Dr. Greg has demonstrated that three Shakespeare quartos dated 1600 and two dated 1608 were actually printed in 1619. The basis of his proof is the watermark.

The fourth evidence is the type with which a book is printed. It is possible to determine when a particular font of type was designed and first cast. We all know the typography of different periods. If a book bears a date earlier than the date of the font, it is forged.

(b) External evidence. The external evidence is that evidence which is outside the text or texts under investigation. The bibliographical evidence is confined to the material of the text and internal evidence to the printed words and their meaning.

The first external evidence is the historical or biographical evidence. If a book was written on a certain date bearing experiences of a certain author and the author belongs to that period, we can say that he is the author of that book. Reversely, if too many books are ascribed to an author we begin to suspect and the doubt increases when it is said that the books were written in two or three months' time.

The second external evidence is an author's statement in one work that he is also the author of another work. Chaucer has given a list of his writings in the Prologue to *The Legend of Good Women* and the *Parson's Tale.*

The third external evidence is a statement by another writer that an author has written a particular book or a number of books.

The fourth external evidence, which is most reliable, is the publisher's record. Most of the publishers maintain a record* of the books and their authors for making payment as royalty. Generally, there is a contract form in which there is the name of the author and his signature. The cash book also is the place where the author's name can be verified.

(c) **Internal evidence.** The Sanskrit classical writers usually wrote at the beginning of their work their name, place and sometimes parentage. Unfortunately this good practice was not observed by the old English writers. They wanted to remain anonymous. However, there are many clues in the text itself with which we can ascribe it to an author.

The first internal evidence is the author's technique and style. Every author's work has unique idiosyncrasies of style. Milton had a Latinate style but Shakespeare the native. It is easy for us to recognise Donne's style and distinguish it from George Herbert's. Versification and vocabulary (poetic diction) are "the two staple categories of stylistic evidence employed in authorship study." Related to style is the technique of the author. Every poet is fond of organising the stanzas in a certain way. He is equally fond of using rhymes. A playwright has a way of beginning and ending a play.

Closely related to the first kind of internal evidence is the subject-matter (content) and the treatment of the theme. Every author has some favourite subject-matter and theme and he repeats them in new forms in many of his works. If a text of

* *Henslow's Diary* is a very famous accounts book. It lists the titles, their authors and money paid to them. The entry of dates is significant.

an unknown authorship is ascribed to an author, a study of the content will reveal whether the attribution is valid or not.

The third is the author's spelling. Many authors are in the habit of spelling certain words in their own way. For example, John Keats had difficulty with the consonant "r" and usually omitted it in his writing. If the letter "r" occurred twice in a word, he would omit it at one place. In words like contrary, striker, retrieve he would omit the first "r" in contrary and striker and second "r" in retrieve. Even in words like strange he sometimes dropped the letter. WB Yeats always made spelling-mistakes and even at his best was not reliable.

Internal evidence is slippery. The researcher must make sure of the validity of his apparatus when he is examining this kind of evidence. In the past, even great scholars were misguided. Some went to the extent of claiming that the author of Shakespeare's plays was Bacon!

But it is certain that when all the three — bibliographical, external and internal — evidences are combined together, they become the most powerful means of verifying authenticity of authorship.

(III) CHRONOLOGY OR DETERMINATION OF DATE

The word chronology, according to Webster's dictionary, means the science of computing time and determining dates. But in literature we use the term with two different meanings. The first meaning is the knowledge of the dates of the most important events of literary significance. The second meaning is the science of determining the dates of events of literary significance. We shall discuss the two aspects of chronology separately under the heads A and B.

A. *The knowledge of date and time relationship.*

It is expected that a research scholar should have a knowledge of the dates when the important literary movements or trends began and the dates when they ended. In English literature different literary trends did not correspond exactly with the beginning and termination of a century although some literary historians have tried to relate them. Literary historians have usually tried to relate a particular trend to the reign of a particular king or queen, especially a queen. There are

Elizabethan writers, Jacobean dramatists, Victorian novelists, Georgian poets etc.

The *Pelican Guide* has divided the periods after the names of the dominant literary figures. But such divisions do not help the research student. He has to make relationship between the important literary events and the dates. For this the student has to do the following at the initial stage :

(a) He should know the three broad divisions of the development of English literature. This division is based upon the development of English language, Old English, Middle English and Modern English.

(i) Old English literature, from the beginnings to the end of the tenth century.

(ii) Middle English literature, from the eleventh century to the end of the fifteenth century.

(iii) Modern English literature, from the sixteenth century to the present age.

(b) This division will give him an idea of the entire literary history, but this is not sufficient He must know the major movements and relate them to the quarters or halves of a century. Although the division into quarter century or half century is not always correct, yet, for a beginner, this is quite useful.

(i) Elizabethan Age : 1550 to 1600 or the second half of the sixteenth century.

(ii) Jacobean Age : 1601 to 1625 or the first quarter of the seventeenth century.

(iii) Restoration Age : 1660 to 1700 or the second half of the seventeenth century.

(iv) Augustan Age : 1701 to 1800 or the eighteenth century.

(v) Romantic Age : 1801 to 1825 or the first quarter of the nineteenth century.

(vi) Victorian Age : 1826 to 1900 or the later three quarters of the nineteenth century.*

(vii) Modern Age : 1901 to the present day.

---

* The Victorian Age ended in 1890 and the period 1891-1900 is called the decadent period. For the sake of convenience the Age has been extended to 1900.

(c) The next step is to associate different writers of the same period. Shakespeare is a dramatist who wrote in both ages, Elizabethan and Jacobean. If we want to remember the dramatists we can divide them into two groups — pre-Shakespearean and post-Shakespearean. It will help us to know their general characteristics and time both. It is also important to know the exact dates of very important events like the publication of *Fairy Queen* (1590) Shakespeare's date of birth (1564), Elizabeth's death (1603), Restoration of Charles II (1660). The Glorious Revolution (1688) the publication of *Lyrical Ballads* (1798) and the crowning of *Queen* Victoria (1832).

(d) Finally, he should prepare a chart for each century in which all the details are given. It is better to list the leading figures of each movement, for example, the University Wits, Metaphysical Poetry, Restoration Tragedy, Restoration Comedy, the Periodical Essayists, the pre-Raphaelites, the Decadents, the Georgians, the Imagists etc.

B. *The science of determining dates.*

The task of the research student, who is already equipped with the knowledge of the time of important literary events, movements and figures, is to determine the date of an undated manuscript. To solve the problem of chronology, we rely on three kinds of evidence : bibliographical, external, and internal.

(a) Bibliographical. Bibliographical evidence consists in the physical material of which the manuscript or printed book is made. We are concerned with the paper, ink and handwriting or print of the text.

(i) *Paper.* It is possible to date a piece of paper. Generally the chief evidence for dating a paper is its watermark. Different paper factories have a record of the watermark. In the Indian context, it should be noted that before independence, most of the paper used for writing and printing purposes was imported from England. The other evidence is the material of the paper. If we take a piece of paper to a papyrologist, he will tell us its date.

Establishing the date of the paper of a manuscript gives us the idea that the writing or printing was done after it. Secondly, the determination of the date of the paper is relevant in the case of that particular copy of the manuscript or edition.

The date of composition may be much earlier. However, the great advantage is that we can convincingly say that the text was written after the date of the manufacture of the paper.

(ii) *Ink*. Ink is the other evidence. A chemist after proper examination can tell us the date of writing. We also know that different kinds of ink were used in the past and they considerably differ from the ink used in modern times. In India, banana juice and soot were mixed and lightly heated to make ink. Gum, water and soot were used to make ink in England. If the date of ink is ascertained, it will give us the knowledge of the exact date of composition of the manuscript.

(iii) *Handwriting*. Paleography helps us in determining the date of the handwriting of a manuscript. Professor R.B. Mckerrow in his book *An Introduction to Bibliography* has given a list of the different shapes of the letters of the English alphabet. The dating of handwriting provides us terminus ante quem (date before which something must have happened) as against the dating of paper which provides terminus a quo (date after which something must have happened).

(iv) *Printing*. In the past the publishers did not print the year of publication nor did they declare the number of the reprint if it was printed for the second or third time. Even if they mentioned the year of publication it was not always correct In India, the same condition is still prevailing and the reason for concealing the number of reprint or impression is just to pocket the money of the royalty to be paid to the author. Related to it are the pirated editions which give a different picture of the date of the first publication.

The best way to date the printed editions is to make a comparison between different editions and reprints and the book that contains the most clean and distinct print is the oldest. The reason for arriving at this conclusion is that the woodcuts used as illustrations or for ornamental initials are intact in the beginning but when they become old they are eaten up at places by worms. Naturally, the later reprints or editions have worm hole marks. In case of metal ornaments, the illustrations in the later editions or impressions are not distinct. The metal after regular use wears out.

(b) External Evidence

(i) The first evidence is reference to an author's work(s) in a book which is dated. The reference provides *terminus ante quem.* Francis Meres has mentioned several plays of Shakespeare in his *Palladis Tamia.* Since this book was published in 1598, we can safely assume that the plays mentioned were written before 1598 and also the books that are not mentioned (the list is long) were written after 1598. It is on this basis we say that *Julius Caesar* and *Hamlet* were written after 1598.

(ii) The second evidence is reference to an author's work or works in his letter to his friends or his friend's to him or other person. Scholars have dated Spenser's "Cantos of Mutability" 1579-80 on the basis of an allusion in a letter written at that time by Gabriel Harvey. A friend's reply to Milton making a reference to the poet's *Of Prelatical Episcopacy* in a letter dated 31 May 1641 provides us *terminus ante quem.*

(iii) The third evidence is provided by the author's biography. If we know the details of his biography and his period, it is possible for us to ascertain the periods of his literary activity. If the author makes a reference to his illness in a work we can say that the text was written after his illness.

(c) Internal Evidence. A close study of the text provides us with the evidences that help us in dating a work.

(i) The first evidence is the occurrence of an allusion to a datable event. These events may be the death of a king, a notable political event, an earthquake or the terrible disease plague. The London Plague was a great event. The reference to the plague in *The Alchemist* gives us the clue to date the play. Dryden's *Absalom and Achitophel* can be dated in the same way. We know the date of the infamous Popish Plot of Titus Oates. The reference to the Dutch attack in *An Essay of Dramatic Poesy* gives us ample evidence to date this work of literary criticism.

(ii) Borrowing is the second internal evidence. An author is not a spider but a bee. He collects materials from different sources, his personal experiences, experiences of his friends, historical events, philosophical ideas, and techniques of his predecessors. Here we are concerned with the datable borrowings.

(iii) An author's technique also helps us to determine his date. Within technique come versification, characterisation, plot construction and ending. It is easy for us to make distinction between an Elizabethan play and a Jacobean play, an early seventeenth century poem and an eighteenth century poem.

(iv) Linguistic evidence, which consists of choice of words, figures of speech, syntactic structures and deviations, is a very solid internal evidence.

Some of the words and phrases that were in use in the seventeenth century are no more used in Modern English. Words like eke, sith, quoth, wend, wot and many more are no longer used now. The pronunciation, too has considerably changed. We learn the pronunciation of some of the words by rhyme. In Pope's time the word "tea" rhymed with "say" and not "see." They have changed semantically too. The word "wife" meant woman upto the time of Shakespeare. Shakespeare used the word "train" to mean tempt and "reform" to revise.

Syntax began to be logical from the time of Dryden. Earlier the clauses were loosely connected. A comparison between Malory's prose and Dryden's prose will show the difference. Bacon's and Milton's prose belong to the transitional period.

While dating a literary work or an author, we have to be a thorough sceptic. Our method should be both inductive and deductive, that is, collection of data, analysis of the arranged items, generalisation on the basis of the discovered facts and application of the principles to a particular text.

(IV) SOURCE STUDY

When we read a poem, a play, or a novel and if we enjoy it, we want to know the events and the people that inspired the creative writer to compose it. After reading Virginia Woolf's *To The Lighthouse* we are eager to know more about Mrs. Ramsay; we want to find out the figure after whom she is modelled. We also ask : are all the events and characters the products of the author's imagination or are they events and people in real life? Source study answers these questions and many more. Besides, source study helps assess the creative writer's artistic power to transmute something ordinary and common into an immortal work of art. The village schoolmaster may have been an ordinary man in real life but his character as depicted in *The Deseted Village* is immortal and the sad story of that ordinary village is the story of all villages. Sometimes source study throws light upon an author's purpose or upon the real meaning and significance of a work or explain an otherwise obscure allusion or expression.

Kinds of sources. Professor Morize recognizes seven kinds of sources.[5]

(i)	Direct sources	:	Legends, histories
(ii)	Documentary sources	:	Readings of the author
(iii)	Sources of detail	:	Plot, characterisation, setting description and figures of speech
(iv)	Composite sources	:	All the sources
(v)	Oral and indefinite sources	:	Ballads, folk-tales
(vi)	Sources of inspiration	:	
(vii)	Graphic and plastic sources	:	Pictures and statues and buildings.

Professor Morize, one of the greatest authorities on literary research, seems to me a bit confusing in his classification. His *composite sources* will include all the sources and so is the case with the sources of inspiration. In fact, it is difficult to accept this classification.

Richard D. Altick classifies them into the following categories :

(i) The people the author knew.
(ii) Visual impressions.
(iii) Graphic representations.
(iv) Combination of sights and sounds.
(v) Contemporary events in which a writer participated or about which he has read.

This classification is incomplete and leaves out many important sources. In my opinion the sources may be classified as under :

(i) Contemporary events and people, including the author.
(ii) Historical events and figures.
(iii) Myths, legends and folk-tales.

(iv) Literary works.

(v) Graphic representations and visual impressions.

(i) Contemporary events and people. A creative writer always lives in the present. Even if he is using a myth or a historical event, he always interprets it in terms of the present. But here we are concerned with the events that moved the author and stirred his imagination. E.M. Forster's *A Passage to India* has its source in the contemporary events and his personal experiences during his sojourn in India. Khuswant Singh's *A Train to Pakistan* and Chaman Nahal's *Azadi* have their source in India's partition and the communal riots that preceded and followed it. The characters in these novels are based upon the real people the authors knew or read about them.

In Chaucer's *Canterbury Tales* there are many characters modelled after the real persons the poet knew. Scholars have discovered that the Sergeant of the Law was Thomas Pynchbeck, The Franklin, Pynchbeck's neighbour, Sir John Bussey of Kesteven in Lincolnshire, The Shipman John Piers, and the Host Henry Bailly, a real innkeeper in Chaucer's time. The eighteenth century writers satirised their adversaries giving them pseudonyms. Now we know these characters as they exist in literary works but a careful research will tell us more how their authors looked at their contemporaries and characterised them.

(ii) Historical events and figures. Creative writers have drawn on history as material for their works. We all know that Shakespeare depended on Plutarch's *Lives* for the Roman plays. The leading figures in his History Plays are all historical. *Macbeth* which is considered to be one of the purest tragedies, has its source in Ralph Holinshed's *Chronicles of England, Scotland, and Ireland* (1577, 1587).[6] A large number of Sir Walter Scott's novels have their source in history. Tolstoy studied history seriously for his *War and Peace* and presented historical events so accurately that historians made corrections in their books of history.

(iii) Myths, legends and folklore. Myths are a perennial source for poets, playwrights and, occasionally, novelists. The myths of Zeus, Aphrodite, Adonis, Pluto, Proserpine, Diana,

Prometheus, Hyperion, have been used by poets and playwrights again and again.* The legends of Hercules, King Arthur and his Round Table, and Robin Hood have attracted many writers. All ballads have their source in folk-lore. It is not that the English writers have confined themselves to the Greek and Roman mythology, they have explored Irish and even Indian and Chinese mythology.

(iv) Literary texts. Homer's *Iliad* and *Odyssey*. Virgil's *Aeneid*, Dante's *Divine Comedy*, Aeschylus' *Oresteia*, Sophocles' *Oedipus* and *The Bible* (we may consider it a piece of literature) have remained inexhaustible source for the English writers. But the list does not end here. Creative writers have drawn on other great works of art for both subject-matter and technique.

Keats's death, no doubt, inspired Shelley to write *Adonais* but for the expression of his feelings he found his material in Bion's *Lament of Aphrodite for Adonis* and Moschus' *Dirge for Bion*. His *Prometheus Unbound* is based on Aeschylus' *Prometheus Bound*. Eugene O'Neill's *Mourning Becomes Electra* and T.S. Eliot's *The Family Reunion* are both based on *Oresteia*.

Writers have looked to great works for technique and versification. The different literary forms, the figures of speech, the metre system, the stanza form all have been studied right from the beginning of poetry and developed from time to time.

(v) Graphic representation. Graphic representation includes pictures and statues and buildings. T.R. Henn has traced the different graphic sources of W.B. Yeats's many poems. Keats's "Ode on a Grecian Urn" was inspired by the Elgin marbles that were brought to the British museum. Wordsworth's "Peele Castle" is another example.

What is more important is the use of graphic representation as an image in a poem or play. In Browning's poetry we have references to many Italian paintings and so do we have in W.H. Auden's poetry. Visual impressions or natural scenes do not need elaboration.

By this classification it should not be assumed that a poet or playwright makes use of only one source in his work. A

* Myth Criticism, which we shall study in the next chapter, systematically analyses how all great works of literature have their source in myths.

work of art is a composite piece and many diverse elements are fused together there. We referred to *Prometheus Unbound* which has its base in Aeschylus' play. But it is also that the verse drama has its immediate source in the French revolution and ultimate source in the myth of Prometheus. The research student, as a rule, should try to discover all the possible sources and explain how the writer has handed the source-material masterfully.

This leads us to the objectives of source study. The main aim is to discover inspiration, material and technique and make distinction between plagiarism and borrowing. Plagiarism is stealing the ideas of other authors and declaring them as one's own. Borrowing is something different. Here the author acknowledges his indebtedness to his source and explains why he is using the source material.

Borrowings can be of two types : conscious and unconscious. Shakespeare's borrowings from Plutarch's *Lives* and Eliot's borrowings from *From Ritual to Romance* and the Elizabethan and Jacobean playwrights are conscious, and Wordsworth's borrowing from Henry Vaughan's "The Retreat" for his "Ode on Intimations of Immortality" and Keats's Miltonic inversions are unconscious.

In all cases it is not much important to lay emphasis on an author's originality or invention but to discover what that writer or his age inherited from the past, how he made improvement upon the previous text or how he interpreted the old characters and past events in the modern context. Edward Bond's *Lear* is surely based upon Shakespeare's *King Lear* but the interpretation of life is different. Our aim therefore is to compare the both and find out the points of departure and explain which one, *Lear* or *King Lear,* is a more successful play.

Technique of Sources Study*

The first step is to discover what books the author owned. There is a difference between an author and a bibliophile. The bibliophile collects books, arranges them and preserves

* The first three points are borrowed from Chauncey Sanders, *The Art of Literary Research*, 188-91.

them in his personal library. It is enough for him that he possesses those books. The author on the other hand buys books to study and use them. It is natural that the books he possesses may have influenced him. But we should not assume that he has studied all the books thoroughly and borrowed from each and every book. However, a visit to his personal library and check of the books is a good starting point.

The second step is to ascertain what newspapers, magazines and journals the author subscribed. A story, an adventure, a description, an anecdote, a new invention, a stirring news may inspire the author to write something. It is also possible that the author himself did not subscribe a periodical but read at his friend's house or in a public library. But in all cases, the knowledge of the subscribed periodicals can help us in discovering the possible source.

The third step is to compile from whatever clues the author has provided us — diary, autobiography, letters, interviews — a list of books he is known to have read. The best starting point is to search the syllabus when he was a student in school and college. He must have read the books that were prescribed in the syllabus. A student reads his text books more attentively and gets inspiration from them. This is a fact that even in our old days we talk about our school and university days with great enthusiasm. It is difficult for an author to escape the uncanny influence of the books he read in his youth.

The fourth step is to find out his literary circle. A literary writer usually is a member of a group of writers sharing almost similar views. If we are in a position to know the aims and creed of his circle, we can find out other sources of his works.

The next step is to study all the other elements in the author's life such as his habits, hobbies, environment, family, friends and places of stay. It is also important to read the works of his friends.

When all done, the final step is to arrange all the materials, examine them carefully, distinguishing fact from fiction to determine what possible sources of the author's works can be.

NOTES

1. Fredson Bowers, *Bibliography and Textual Criticism,* (Oxford : Clarendon Press, 1964), 26-27.
2. All these are collected in *Evidence in Literary Scholarship,* ed., Rene Wellek and Alvaro Ribeiro (Oxford : Charendon Press, 1979).
3. Fredson Bowers, "Textual Criticism," The *Aims and Methods of Scholarship,* 33.
4. Richard D. Altick, *The Art of Literary Research,* 63.
5. Quoted, Chauncey Sanders, *The Art of Literary Research,* 172.
6. HJC Grierson, Introduction, *Macbeth* (Oxford : The Charendon Press, 1914), xiii.

6

Methods of Research : Critical Approaches and Theories

The methods of research — biography, bibliography and textual criticism — we discussed in the previous chapters are methods of research in literary history. The method that we are going to discuss is concerned with the analysis, interpretation and evaluation of the works of an author. A training in literary criticism enables the research student to read a text independently and make distinction between a good work of art and a bad work of art. In the twentieth century, literary criticism has advanced so much that it is important for the research student to have a good knowledge of different approaches and theories of literature. Realising the problems of the students of literature Wilbur Scott edited an anthology[1] of modern critical texts dividing them into five broad groups — The Moral Approach, The Psychological Approach, The Sociological Approach, The Formalistic Approach and the Archetypal Approach — with a short introduction to each approach. In the Argument he stated the purpose of the anthology :

In my teaching experience, I have concluded that the student who knows he has things to say about a work of literature, but has no direction by which to shape his perceptions, finds his problem solved by taking on the discipline and organisation of one of the five approaches used here.[2]

Soon after the publication of Scott's *Five Approaches of Criticism* the academies of the USA realised the value of acquainting the students of literature with the main approaches and critical theories of the twentieth century. William J. Handy and Max Westbrook edited a more comprehensive Reader[3] in 1974 and divided the essays into six broad groups : Formalist Criticism, Genre Criticism, Archetypal Criticism, Psycho-analytic Criticism, Historical Criticism and Interdisciplinary Criticism. In the Preface they wrote :

Our chief hope is that these selections and this arrangement will help the student to see and to be responsible for the theoretical implications of what he says about the meaning of a word in a poem, that is, to become a more perceptive reader.[4]

The eminent British critic David Lodge edited *20th Century Criticism : A Reader* (1980) and *Modern Criticism and Theory* (1988), both published by Longman, with the purpose of making students aware of the philosophy behind each critical approach and theory. The great quality of these two anthologies is that they are not confined to the British and American critics only and have included Marxist Criticism, Structuralism, Russian Formalism and Post-structuralism.

The main purpose of referring to these Readers is that students in India must know what approach they are taking while doing research on an author or age and if they remain ignorant of the main approaches, they will confuse one modern critic with another and in this confusion may produce a doctoral dissertation which will be a muddle. The main theories of literature to me are : New Criticism, Psycho-analytic criticism, Myth Criticism, Marxist Criticism and Structuralism, Post-structuralism (including Deconstruction) and Feminist Criticism.

(I) NEW CRITICISM

New Criticism has its roots in the critical theories of T.S. Eliot and I.A. Richards. Taking cue from the French critic-poet Remy de Gourment, Eliot propounded the impersonal theory of art in his famous essay "Tradition and the Individual Talent" and asserted the independent existence of poetry. He compared the poet to a catalyst, a medium, that combines emotions and feelings together to make poetry. In "Dante and Shakespeare" he refuted the idea held by older critics that a great philosophy makes a poem or play great. In the Introduction to the 1928 edition of the *Sacred Wood* he defined his notion of the autonomy of poetry and art :

We can only say that a poem, in some sense, has its own

life; that its parts form something quite different from a body of neatly ordered biographical data; that the feeling or emotion, or vision, resulting from the poem is something different from the feeling or vision in the mind of the poet.[5]

I.A. Richards, too, maintained the independent entity of poetry and, after his experiments with the undergraduate students at Cambridge University, came to the conclusion that the disclosure of the author's name distorts our understanding of his works. He, therefore, suggested that we can best understand a poem if we pay full attention to its sense, feeling, tone and intention. The other significant contribution of his to literary criticism is the distinction between scientific truth and poetic truth. Science, he said, makes statement and poetry pseudo-statement. The "truth" of a scientific statement can be verified in a laboratory but the "truth" of the pseudo-statement depends upon our feelings and attitude. Related to it is his distinction between two kinds of language, referential and emotive, the first the language of science and the latter of poetry.

Eliot and Richards together evoked responses from the American critics who, largely accepting their new poetics and textual analysis made certain corrections and evolved a new critical approach to literature, which is now universally known as New Criticism.

John Crowe Ranson criticised in *The New Criticism* the affective theory of I.A. Richards, especially his notion of synaesthesia and levelled the same charge against T.S. Eliot. He found Richards's relevant poetic structure not only hypothetical but also highly subjective; for if the balanced poise is in our response, not in the structure of the poem, our analysis will certainly be erroneous and whimsical. In *The World's Body* he discussed the poetic structure in detail and argued that a poem has the *logical structure,* which is its argument, and the *irrelevant local texture* which is its imagery, metaphor, symbolism and other local details that make the poem a rich composite. Poetry therefore, is not purely a pseudo-statement; the logical structure contains some scientific truth and hence objectivity.

The principles Ransom laid down in *The New Criticism*

and *The World's Body* became the starting point for all modern American critics and the concept that a poem has its own entity* and that in our analysis we should go from its structure to meaning, not vice-versa.

However, the New Critics soon split into two groups, one following the philosophy of Kant and Coleridge and the other of Aristotle. Following the classification of Handy and Westbrook, the first group will be called the Formalist critics and the second Genre Critics or neo-Aristotelians.

(a) Formalist criticism. YvorWinters, R.P. Blackmur, Robert Heilman. Allen Tate and Cleanth Brooks followed Ransom's philosophical aesthetics which is based upon the aesthetics of the great German philosopher Immanuel Kant. These critics have negated the Victorian and neohumanist emphasis on the moral uses of literature, the historical tradition and the biography of the author. They have also refuted Roger Fry's concept of pure form and regarded poetry as a valid source of knowledge that cannot be communicated in terms other than its own.

What is important for the formalist critic is a close reading of the text in terms of its form (metre, stanza form, rhyme and rhythm) and the materials (simile, metaphor, image, allusion, symbol) it is made of because it is the concretum of the logical structure and irrelevant local texture. The method of analysis is like that of G. Wilson Knight, F.R. Leavis, L.C. Knights and William Empson.

Cleanth Brooks deviated from John Crow Ransom in his approach to poetry. Ransom and Winters held that the logical or cognitive aspect of poetic apprehension was necessary because a poem contains scientific truth but Brooks maintained that a poem is an organic composition of its images. Secondly, praising I.A. Richards's emphasis on the use of irony, he redefined irony that it is "the obvious warping of a statement by the context" and maintained that irony or paradox is the principle of the poetic structure. He demonstrated his method of analysis in *Understanding Poetry* (1938) and *Understanding Fiction* (1943) written in collaboration with Robert Penn Warren,

---

* Archibald Macleish's dictum "A poem should not mean, but be" gained wide popularity.

and *Understanding Drama* (1945) with Robert Heilman. He made the exposition of the theory in the essay "The Formalist Critic" (1951) which made the younger critics and historian name the New Criticism Formalist Criticism. His method of analysis is so penetrating, exhaustive and powerful that it is yet to be surpassed by scholars and critics in the UK and the USA and no student of literature can spare himself from studying the three mentioned books.

(b) Genre critics or the neo-Aristotelians. Handy and Westbrook have named the criticism practised by the Chicago School of critics, on the ground that "any critic who concentrates on formal distinction in literature may be called, in the loose sense of the term, a Genre Critic," but soon they hasten to add "the study of Genre Criticism, in any sense of the term, is best begun with a study of Aristotle and of their use of the inductive method as a foundation for literary criticism." In my opinion the Genre Critics* come under the broader group of the New Critics and, as we shall see later on, they have differed with Ransom on certain subtle points and with Brooks on the principles underlying his method of analysis. It is better to call the Chicago School of Critics* neo-Aristotelians because they have their base in Aristotle's philosophy and his method of analysis.

Elder Olson in his classic essay "The Poetic Method of Aristotle : Its Powers and Limitations" has given the best interpretation, at least to me, of Aristotle *Poetics*. Placing *Poetics* in the general scheme of Aristotle's philosophy, Olson proves that the art of poetry is a productive science, mathematics a theoretical science and politics a practical science. Aristotle made this division of knowledge using both inductive and deductive methods, the same method the Greek philosopher applied for identification and classification of the productive sciences. He divided the fine arts on the basis of medium, object, mode and function and declared that the artist is a maker. In imitating things he makes something new. For example, a sculptor in making a marble statue imitates the human form but the statue he has made is neither a human

* The leading critics are R.S. Crane, Elder Olson, Wayne C Booth and John Mckeon.

being nor a piece of marble : it is a work of art and has a structure of its own. Since all its parts are proportionate to their function and form a whole which, too in relation to its parts is proportionate in size and hence beautiful.

After interpreting Aristotle's *Poetics* and his method thus the neo-Aristotelians under the leadership of R.S. Crane have criticised Cleanth Brooks on two grounds. The first is that the Formalist critic's method is, because he has already taken it for granted that irony or paradox is the principle of structure, deductive, whereas a critic should use both inductive and deductive methods and start his analysis of the given text using the inductive method first. The second argument and this is more important and equally valid, is that the Formalist critics do not make distinction between two genres of literature. Even two texts of the same genre are not alike. For example, *Othello* and *Macboth* both tragedies and both written by Shakespeare are quite different. *Othello* is on the pattern of the Greek tragedy as defined by Aristotle but *Macboth* is a play between *Othello* and *Richard III;* the latter could be very well rejected by Aristotle on moral grounds. No critic can do justice to *Macboth* unless he defines its place in the history of tragedy, differentiates with other tragedies, and then analyses it first inductively and then deductively to understand its structure, and the way the author has organised it. The basic difference between the Formalists and the Neo-Aristotelians lies in their principles of critical method and nature of art. The neo-Aristotelians follow the great Greek philosopher when they state that knowledge is based on systematic analysis. The subject under study may seem or even be irregular but the study must be systematic and principled, *i.e.*, scientific. It follows then that literature which is a product of imagination may be subjective hence partly wayward but its study, criticism must be scientific. The Formalist, on the other hand, says that the study of poetry should be ontological, not scientific.

Secondly, the Formalist who follows Kant's "The Thing-in-itself," believes that knowledge can be derived from the poem and the poem alone which is under study. The neo-Aristotelian says that the knowledge of a thing cannot be discovered within the framework of the thing itself. The adequate knowledge of a thing, thereby a literary work, can be gained when we place it in the system in which it exists.

However, these differences, although fundamental and of far-reaching consequences, are made on the philosophical or ideological plane; in practice both employ the same technique.*

(II) PSYCHO-ANALYTIC CRITICISM

Psycho-analytic criticism has its origin in Sigmund Freud's psychology. Freud's significant contribution to literature and literary criticism is his concept of the "unconscious." He explained that man's psyche has two parts : the conscious and the unconscious. The unconscious for Freud is the reservoir of the repressed feelings censored by the conscious. Later on, he revised his ideas on the nature of psyche and used four technical terms : *Libido, id, ego* and *super ego. Libido* is the primary source of energy and is sexual; *id* is the unconscious and *ego* is the conscious personality that mediates between the unconscious and the *super ego,* conscience, which is the total sum of the social norms. Any libidinous behaviour or desire that goes against the standard social norms arouses a sense of guilt in the doer and s/he becomes neurotic. It is also that the tabooed desire is censored and repressed by the super ego. This repressed desire or the sense of guilt produced by the tabooed act finds place in the *id* or the unconscious. The unconscious is active when ego and super ego are asleep. Dreams and reveries are the manifestations of the activities of the unconscious or *id*; they are the "displacement" of reality and a kind of wish-fulfilment.

Freud's views on art and creative writers is a part of his psycho-analysis. He considers the creative writer a kind of neurotic, who fails to come to terms with reality and takes solace in his reverie or fantasy where his wishes are fulfilled. Here he is guided by the pleasure principle which is constructive, not death principle which is destructive.

In his classical essay "Creative Writers and Daydreaming" Freud traces the sources of a writer's work and explains how s/he manages to make an impression on the readers.

---

* See Elder Olson's analysis of W.B. Yeats's "Sailing to Byzantium" and Cleanth Brooks's of "Ode on a Grecian Urn."

The sources generally are his/her personal experiences structured on the pattern of myths and folk-tales which are illustrative material of basic human instincts, conflicts and yearnings. The myths of Oedipus, Electra, Narcissus, Persephone Demeter, and Adonis, for example, are the manifestations of man's basic instincts and conflicts.

Coming to the creative process, Freud says that the writer is a kind of neurotic; the difference between the two is that the neurotic has no control over the unconscious but the writer, though unable to cope with the reality, can control it. Man is imaginative by nature and his imaginal activity can be traced back to his childhood. The child at play imagines the objects (say, toys) to be real and humanizes them. It takes the play seriously. We can say that the play is a displacement of reality. Just as father is the master of the house, the child is the master of the toy-world.

The creative writer does the same as the child at play. He takes the world of his reverie (fantasy) seriously. This world of fantasy is a displacement of reality. The creative writer, crushed under the heavy burden of life, a world of fantasy with intense seriousness he once carried on his games in childhood. There he can win the high yield of pleasure by equating the serious occupations of today with his childhood games and throw off the too heavy burden. No one can give up a pleasure once s/he has experienced. Man who has derived immense pleasure from play in his childhood can not do so in his manhood. He gives it up and picks up its substitute, fantasy or day-dream.

But he cannot tell his fantasy to others. It is easy for him to confess his misdeeds. Being torn between the opposites of fantasy and reality, he modifies it to reveal it to others. Just as by confessing our guilt we get cured of the sickness of our spirit, the writer by revealing his modified fantasy gets cured of his nervous illness.

All people do not fantasy; only the unsatisfied ones do, and this is because the motives of fantasies are unsatisfied wishes, and every single fantasy is the fulfilment of a wish. A wish can be an ambitious wish which will serve to elevate the subject's personality or an erotic one to gain the object of love. Sometimes both the wishes are intertwined.

The fantasies are not stereotyped nor are they unalterable; they are shifting and their relation to time is very important. There are three moments of time : present, past and future. Fantasies are first aroused by the current impressions, the provoking occasions that arouse one of the subject's major wishes. Then the creative writer looks back to a memory of past experience (an infantile one, usually) in which this wish was fulfilled and, finally, creates a situation related to the future which represents a fulfilment of the wish.

To illustrate his viewpoint Freud gives the example of a poor orphan boy employed in some house or firm fantasies his marriage to the employer's only beautiful girl and succession of his property. We can take the example of Dickens's *David Copperfield.*

A friend's remark that he was helped by a man when he was employed in his teens, arouses the painful experience. Dickens looks back to the past and creates a situation relating to the future fulfilling his wish to be an established writer. He modifies the fantasy by patterning it on a fairy tale in which an ugly old woman like Miss Betsey helps an orphan boy. The ugly woman, in fact, is a fairy in disguise. Miss Betsey functions like a fairy in *David Copperfield.* Similarly, W.B. Yeats's poem "When You are Old," is a kind of wish fulfilment. He imagines his beloved repent for rejecting his sincere love in her old age, a time when she is past love.

Freud further says that the biography of an author is of great value to understand and interpret his or her writings. For this it is always better to choose the lesser writers. The lesser writer chooses a hero who is the centre of interest and for whom he tries to win our sympathy by every possible means and places him under the special protection of Providence. All the women in the novel invariably fall in love with the hero. All the characters are sharply divided into the good and the bad, the former supporting the hero and the latter his adversary.

To sum up, a strong impression/experience of the present awakens in the writer a memory of his early experience (usually infantile) from which there now proceeds a wish which finds its fulfilment in his created work. The created work, like a daydream, is a continuation of, and a substitute for, what was once the play of childhood. He usually handles a readymade material, available in the popular treasure house of myths, legends and fairy or folk tales.

We experience a great pleasure in a novel, a short story or a poem because he softens the character of his egoistic day dreams by altering and disguising it and gratifies us by the aesthetic yield of pleasure which he offers in the presentation of his fantasies.

Freud analysed Shakespeare's *Hamlet, Macbeth, A Midsummer Night's Dream* and *King Lear* in brief, wrote a brilliant essay on Dostoevsky's *Brothers Karmazov* and a full length study *Delusion and Dream* of the novel *Gradiva* by Wilhelm Jensen of Denmark.

Psycho-analytic criticism, after Freud, has had two main trends : writing of an author's biography and analysis of texts. The term *psycho-biography* is now being used for those biographies that focus on the psychological development of an author. Sir Herbert Read is the first such critic who has written a biographical criticism of Wordsworth. The other critics in this category are Eric H. Erickson (*Young Man Luther* 1958), Leon Edel (Henry James 5 volumes (1952-73) and the different writers in the series *Writers and Their World* which includes biographies of Mark Twain, Jane Austen, E.M. Forster, Virginia Woolf and other important writers.

The analysis of literary texts, after Freud, began with Dr. Ernest Jones (*Hamlet and Oedipus*). Derek Traversi followed him with the essay on Jane Austen "The Regulated Hatred." In recent times the important critics are Marie Bonabarte, Norman Holland, Norman Brown, and the greatest of them all Jacques Lacan.

Apart from these critics, Freud's psycho-analytic criticism has influenced the creative writers most. Lawrence, Auden, Sylvia Plath, Eugene O'Neill and the post-modern writers have consciously or unconsciously adopted Freud's psycho-analysis. Among the critics, the post-structuralists and the feminists have partly accepted Freud's ideas but rejected and rightly so, his absurd notions of Oedipus complex, Narcissism and "the Lack," But his greatest and soundest critic is his disciple C.G. Jung.

(III) MYTH CRITICISM

Myth criticism, also called archetypal criticism, is one of the most recent critical theories of literature. Like Formalist Criticism it uses all the methods of structural analysis and like Genre Criticism it accepts the development of different genres, but its main emphasis is on the cultural and psychological pattern that underlies a literary work. "In every age," says Northrop Frye,

> Poets who are thinkers (remembering that poets think in metaphors and images, not in propositions) and are deeply concerned with the origin or destiny or desires of mankind — with anything that belongs to the larger outlines of what literature can express — can hardly find a literary theme that does not coincide with a myth.[6]

The main objective of the myth critic is to trace the thematic relationship between a literary work and the original myth which is its source and to explain why creative writers have taken and are taking great interest in ancient myths. When he does it successfully, he makes us able "to understand the corresponding place that a work of literature has in the context of literature as a whole."[7]

Myth criticism owes its origin to the works of anthropologists Edward Tylor and James Frazer and psychologists Sigmund Freud and Carl Jung who after an intensive analysis of the ancient myths arrived at the conclusion that myths are to be taken seriously and that they are essentially primitive man's explanation of the phenomena of nature (the anthropological approach), the projections of the desires repressed and collected in the unconscious (the psycho-analytic approach), or the manifestations of the archetypes of the collective unconscious (Jung's analytical approach).

Before Tylor and Frazer, Giambadista Vico had scientifically analysed the Greek, Roman and other European myths and found in them clues of the consciousness of remote civilisations and cultures. After explaining man's cultural and intellectual history he arrived at the conclusion that the gods and heroes of the ancient societies are the expressions of human nature and behaviour. Vico's interpretation of myths and mythical figures is very near to that of Freud; Vico held that man creates god out of fear and projects his troublesome desires on gods, and Freud concluded that "in the legend, a human desire is transformed into a divine privilege." The difference between the two is that Vico, being a social scientist, laid emphasis on the social customs and institutions which have developed out of the human beliefs and desires that myths disclose.

Professor Gilbert Murray, perhaps, the first myth critic, analysed some of the classics of European literature in the light of Frazer's thesis propounded in *The Golden Bough.** In the essay "Hamlet and Orestes," he, after a comparative study of the classical Greek literature, Saxo's *History of the Danes,* especially the Amlodi or Amlehtus saga, Shakespeare's *Hamlet* and the ancient Greek myth of Zeus' birth, arrived at the conclusion that Hamlet, Orestes, Gertrude, Clytemnestra, Agamemmon and Laius are the vegetative deities and they have their origin in the rituals of the death and revival of the vegetative gods. After establishing relationship between Orestes and Hamlet, Gertrude and Clytemnestra and Claudius and Aegisthus, he commented :

There is clearly a common element in all these stories, and the reader will doubtless have recognised it. It is the world wide ritual story of what we may call the Golden-Bough kings. That ritual story is, as I have tried to show elsewhere,** the fundamental conceptions that form the basis of Greek tragedy, and not Greek tragedy only.[8]

In other words Clytemnestra, Jocasta and Gertrude are Earth Mother, Agamemnon, Laius and King Hamlet are the dying-god (King-year), and Orestes, Oedipus and Hamlet have the elements of winter in them.

Although Freud maintained that the creative writer makes use of the "popular treasure house of myths, legends and fairy-tales" for the structure of his work and myths are "distorted vestiges of the wishful fantasies of whole nations, the secular dreams of youthful humanity," he never considered myths as the expression of social reality and their purpose and meaning serious and instructive.

---

* For the influence of Frazer's monumental work on creative writers and literary critics, see Vickery, *The Impact of the Golden Bough.*

** *Euripides and His Age* (1913).

Freud's interpretation of myths was blinkered by the narrowness of his notion of the unconscious. C.G. Jung, differing with his teacher, commented :

For Freud, accordingly, the unconscious is of an exclusively personal nature, although he was aware of its archaic and mythological thought forms.[9]

He pointed out that our unconscious has two layers, the superficial or personal and the deeper or the collective; the personal unconscious rests upon the collective unconscious which is inborn and universal. In contrast to the personal psyche, the collective unconscious has contents and modes of behaviour that are more or less the same everywhere and in all individuals.[10] He went on to say that whereas the contents of the personal unconscious are chiefly the feeling-toned complexes constituting the personal and private side of life, the contents of the collective unconscious are the archetypes which find their expression in dreams, myths, fairy-tales and folk-lore. The archetypes are the experiences of the race stored in the collective unconscious which is like a pool of water and when the individual has a complete breakdown in his personal life and is unable to adjust himself with the present situation, the collective unconscious, the store house of the racial wisdom comes to his rescue. The archetypes are altered by becoming conscious and by being perceived and they take their colour from the individual consciousness in which they happen to appear. Jung emphasised the point that it is not important what the primitive man saw in the physical world but how he saw it. The archetypes that were formed during the early history of our race are all present in the collective unconscious of ours. We being members of a community or race are guided by both personal and collective unconscious. The artist, too, accordingly in his creative process is guided by not only his personal experiences but also the racial experiences. Contrary to the conclusion of Freud that an artist is a neurotic, Jung considers him to be a representative of humanity who expresses in his literary work the experiences and wisdom of his ancestors :

As a human being he may have moods and a will and personal aims, but as an artist he is "man" in a higher sense, he is "collective" man — one who carries and shapes the unconscious, psychic life of mankind.[11]

It is therefore useless to look into the personal life of the artist for the explication of his work; art, in fact, forces upon him and he is only an efficient cause.

After the pioneering works of Vico, Tylor, Frazer, Freud and Jung, myth criticism came to its own in the critical works of Gilbert Murray, Maud Bodkin, Leslie Fiedler, Richard Chase, Northrop Frye and Lilian Feder who combined both anthropology and psychology.

Maud Bodkin* explained why certain symbols and images, simple though they may appear, move us more deeply than the other symbols. Her analysis of Coleridge's *Rime of Ancient Mariner* and Dante's *Divine Comedy* lucidly explains their enduring emotive power by testing them for the presence of archetypal motifs which express the most profound and universal experiences and concerns of the human race.

Northrop Frye, the greatest theoretician of myth criticism, has combined Aristotle, Freud, Frazer and Jung all together. According to him literature is "an imitation of infinite social action and infinite human thought, the mind of a man who is all men, the universal creative word which is all words."[12] He argues that only archetypal and anagogic criticism can fully explain the nature, origin and form of literature. Literary criticism, he says, is like the physical sciences which systematically study nature and try to explain order in it, interpreting apparently diverse phenomena which are governed by certain laws that operate systematically and regularly. Literary criticism must be systematic to find out a system in literature. He very emphatically asserts that "criticism cannot be systematic unless there is a quality in literature which enables it to be so, an order of words corresponding to the order of nature in the natural sciences.[13] What, we may ask, is the quality in literature that puts an order in it? Frye's answer is that the archetype is the unifying force and it is the task of

* Bodkin's *Archetypal Patterns in Poetry* (Oxford Univ. Press, 1934) did not draw attention when it was first published but now has received its due recognition and is considered one of the pioneering works of myth criticism. Bodkin herself was a disciple of Jung.

the literary critic to explain the structure of literature, its origin and development, and the reason for the recurrent return of the creative writers to certain figures and themes. In order that he should best analyse the structure of a text he has to go back to its archetype, the primordial images, that are expressed through myths, legends, folk-tales and rituals.

The primitive man saw a pattern in the cycle of day and night, of seasons, and of human life and identified morning with spring and childhood, noon with the summer season and manhood, evening with autumn and old age, and night with winter and death. In order to overcome the challenges of nature he constructed "a central narrative around a figure who is partly the sun, partly vegetative fertility and partly a god or archetypal human being."[14] The central myth, therefore, is the quest myth in which the hero represents the aspirations of the entire community and in his triumph or defeat lies the comic or tragic vision of the people. From this central myth have stemmed the myths related to the four phases of man's life, the four phases of the sun and the four seasons of the year. The different genres of literature have their origin in the myths in which archetypes have found expression.

Frye and other myth critics are critical of the Formalist critics who analyse a literary work isolating it from its social and cultural background. According to them literature is essentially a social product and in order that we can understand its nature, function and purpose we must go back to the archetypes of the collective unconscious which have found their expression in myths, folk-tales and legends of the community.

(IV) MARXIST CRITICISM

Marxist Criticism has its origin in the writings of Karl Marx and Frederick Engels who interpreted the structure of society and the laws of social development that are responsible for the progress of civilisation. The great problem, they thought, was how man progressed from the hunting stage to the stage of modern civilisation and what forces worked behind this progress. In their opinion the economic forces, man's need of food, clothes and shelter, impelled him to constantly improve his tools of production. The social group that was more successful in improving its tools of production became more advanced. Besides, Marx and Engels observed that law, religion and government in a society differed from the other societies if the tools of production were different in nature. On this basis, they divided the structure of society into the base structure consisting of productive forces, tools of production and mode of production, in other words man's material activity which is primary, and the superstructure, consisting of law, religion, politics, philosophy and literature, man's higher forms of activity.

The base structure determines the contents of the superstructure. In other words, if there is a change in the tools and mode of production, the whole structure of the society is changed and people begin to think in a new way. But this does not mean that the superstructure is always passive; on the other hand it, too, has its effects on the base structure. The progress of civilisation has not been straightforward. Once man crossed the hunting stage and reached the agricultural stage, the society got divided into two broad classes, one class controlling the means of production and the other deprived of it. The deprived class began to struggle for the control of the means of production, sometimes covertly and sometimes openly. The thinking and conceiving of the deprived class was quite different from those of the ruling class that had economic power in its hands. Thus the known history, Marx concluded, is the history of class-struggle. He corrected Hegel's Idealistic philosophy by his material conception of the world and said that the progress of society is certainly dialectical but it is matter, not idea, which is primary; matter came first and idea followed it. If we want to study the nature, origin and function of law, religion, government or literature our approach should be sociological-historical. We first should study the structure of society at a given time and know its historical development how it reached the present state and what forces worked behind it. Literature is to be studied in both sociological and historical terms.

Literature, according to Marxist critics, being a part of the superstructure is continually modified by the changes in the base structure brought about by improvement in the tools of production. Because it is dependent on the material activity of man, it will be wrong to say that it is a divine gift or imitation of reality as Plato conceived it. Literature is basically a creative reproduction of reality. The writer born in a particular period of society has certain experiences and those experiences make him study the underlying reality of the social events and interpret it in his individual way. Since literature is not a science or social science, the writer presents that reality by creating a world of imagination which is not quite different from the world we live in.[15]

Secondly, literature like art is a product of labour. In the beginning of history, man's hand was very much like that of an ape but became more and more flexible after he started making tools for his living. In the constant effort of improving the tools the hand became not only the organ of labour but also the product of labour. The folk-tales, legends and ancient hymns have originated from man's material activity, *i.e.*, labour. Natural events like the cycle of seasons, the diurnal course, the four seasons of man's life, waxing and waning of the moon affected his material life. Naturally birth, marriage, death, the advent of the spring and rainy seasons, periods of plantation and harvest were the momentous events in his life and he accordingly celebrated festivals and performed rituals associated with these events. Through myths he sought the explanation of different natural events, composed hymns to please the forces of nature which controlled his material life and patterned the tune and rhythm of the songs to "the rhythmical movement of human bodies engaged in collective labour."[16]

Thirdly, changes in content and form of literature are brought about by the changes in the material base. The development of literature, the rise and wane of a genre or form can be interpreted scientifically in terms of the laws of social development. Since the day man progressed from the stage of primitive communism, there has been a fierce competition among different classes for the control over the means of production. The class that won the battle, controlled the economic structure and thereby the superstructure. It imposed its ideas on the rest of the society and made laws, created religion, evolved a political system to serve its interest. In literature and art the same ideology worked. However, the other classes, the ruled and exploited, continuously struggled for the control over the means of production. Once the ruled class gained the economic power, it began to assert its own ideas and these new ideas came in conflict with the old ideas, the ideas of the declining class. Later on, the new ideas became the dominant ideas of the epoch and were reflected in law, religion, metaphysics and literature of the age.[17] Yet, it would be a vulgar representation of Marxism to say straightway that the development of literature is solely dependent on the laws of social development. Literature being a specific form of social consciousness has its own laws of development. Krylov has very succinctly summarised this view of Marx and Engels :

They were in no way inclined to qualify art as a passive product of the economic system. On the contrary, they emphasised that the various forms of social consciousness — including, of course, artistic-creation — actively influence the social reality from which they emerge.[18]

The other reason, and this is equally important, is the role of the individual creativity. The artist in the words of Pakinson is not "a passive reflector of social consciousness,"[19] he has his own world outlook and way of representing it. It is not necessary for him to be a follower of the ruling ideas of the age; he may be critical of them and may posit the ideas that are advanced of his age. Here, Marxist criticism goes ahead of the old Historical criticism represented by Hippolyte-Taine who maintained that a work of literature is the product of the race, milieu and the moment. Marxist criticism rejects this mechanistic view of history and literature and presents the dialectical view.

Fourthly, Marxist criticism lays stress on the correlation between reality and artistic truth. Artistic truth is reality presented in a special way. The writer must be a truthful observer of life and present it in all its details because the truth discovered by a creative writer and a scientist or social scientist is always the same. In fact, as Novikov has said, while considering the question of artistic truth and the general laws of nature it is necessary to combine both the interests of science and art. The artistic truth should be seen in the content, not in technique because a work of art is the gist of the artist's interpretation of reality and is inseparably associated with the art of realism.

Finally, in Marxist criticism, realism and socialist realism are the two terms which need some explanation. Engels defined the term realism in his letter to Margaret Harkness :

Realism to my mind implies besides truth of detail, the truthful reproduction of typical characters in typical circumstances.

At other place he explained the term type :

In both spheres the characters exhibit the sharp individuation so customary in your [Minna Kautsky's] work. Each of them is a type, but at the same time also a definite individual, a Deiser (this one) as old Hegel would say, and that is how it should be.[20]

Maxim Gorky used the terms critical realism and socialist realism. According to him socialist realism is the heir of critical realism. The literature of critical realism was born when the bourgeois system was declining under the pressure of contradictions in society and socialist realism when the proletariat became strong enough to challenge the power of the bourgeoisie. Arnold Kettle has defined critical realism :

It is the literature written in the era of class society, from a point of view which while not fully socialist, is nevertheless sufficiently critical of class society to reveal important truth about that society and to contribute to the freeing of human consciousness from the limitations which class society has imposed upon it.[21]

Socialist realism is the most recent trend in the development of literature. It as defined by Arnold Kettle, is literature written from the point of view of the class-conscious working class, whose socialist consciousness illuminates their whole view of the nature of the world and of the potentialities of mankind.[22]

The Marxist critics who follow the Russian school use the term critical realism but of the European school led by Georg Lakacs and followed in England by Terry Eagleton and Raymond Williams prefer the term realism. However, both the schools agree that realism began to shape in the beginning of the nineteenth century in the works of Tolstoy, Balzac, Dickens, George Eliot, Henrik Ibsen and Gustav Flaubert. These novelists faithfully depicted the contradictions in society and presented solutions to the problems plaguing the common people so that it would be a society where there would not be wide gaps between two persons. Socialist realism began to shape at the moment of the collapse of the old capitalist order towards the end of the nineteenth century. Its emergence coincided with the proletariat struggle against the bourgeoisie, the oppressed people's struggle against the imperialists and colonialists.

The eminent writers of socialist realism are Maxim Gorky, Mayakovsky, Sholokhov, Prem Chand, Bernard Shaw, Pablo Neruda, Bertolt Brecht and John Steinbeck.

Marxist criticism analyses a literary text and evaluates an author from a new point of view which is content-oriented. Its emphasis is on the presentation and analysis of social reality and the author's world vision. It makes us aware of the fact that a lesser writer always presents his class interest and only a great writer rises above his personal and class interests and creates in his work a world or at least hints at such a world where there is no exploitation and where men and women enjoy untrammelled freedom.

(V) STRUCTURALISM AND POST-STRUCTURALISM

Theory. Structuralism and Post-structuralism both came to England and America almost simultaneously. In the forties T.S. Eliot, I.A. Richards, F.R. Leavis, William Empson, John Crowe Ransom, R.P. Blackmur, Cleanth Brooks and Allen Tate were the dominating figures and no one cared to see what was happening in the Continent. The New Criticism, mildly challenged and partly modified by the Neo-Aristotelians, continued to dominate even in the seventies. By the time the British and the American academics came to realise the value of Structuralism, it was already in decline and was being replaced by Post-structuralism. Structuralism depended heavily for its principles on linguistics and anthropology. The British and the American critics had never thought in this way. Bodkin, of course, had written *Archetypal Patterns in Poetry* and William Empson *Seven Types of Ambiguity* but they had no idea of modern linguistics or modern anthropology and therefore, when structuralism came to the island it created a stir. Structuralism soon developed into Post-structuralism because, the modern critics enriched criticism by their knowledge of psychoanalysis, philosophy and Marxism and made it a theory.*

What follows in this brief introduction is an account of the basic concepts of structuralism and post-structuralism and practice of post-structuralism.

Structuralism has its origin in Ferdinand de Saussure's *Course in General Linguistics* published posthumously in 1915. De Saussure made distinction between *langue* and *parole* and defined language as a structured system. He pointed out that the relationship between sound pattern (signifier) and conception (signified) is arbitrary and, therefore, the linguistic sign, combination of signifier and signified is arbitrary. It is this arbitrariness of the linguistic signs that necessitates a scientific study of language. Since language is a part of social life he conceived of a science, semiology, which will study the role of signs as part of social life and "the laws which semiology will discover will be laws applicable in linguistics." The other important discovery of Saussure is that he proved that speech is primary and writing is its tangible form and that we understand a word or a sentence because it is so structured.

What does structure mean then? We may ask. The modern linguist's answer is that it is the internal relationship between the signs of a language. We know that the words "eat" and "tea" are different, although both the words contain the same sounds (phonemes). The difference is due to difference in the structure of the two words; the phonemes do not occur in the same order. In the same way words are ordered to form sentences in a language. Two sentences differ in meaning because they have two different structures. Ferdinand De Saussure explained the meaning of structure by his famous example of the game of chess. If wooden chessmen are replaced by ivory chessmen, there will not be any effect on the grammar of chess, but if we increase or decrease their number, the change will have a profound effect on the game. This internal

---

* David Lodge writes : In the process, literary criticism has been drawn into the vortex of a powerful new field of study in which all these disciplines are merged and interfused and which goes under the general name of theory. David Lodge, "Foreword" *Modern Criticism and Theory*, ed., David Lodge (London and New York: Longman, 1988), ix.

relationship between the chessmen is the structure of the game. Thus for the structuralists, in the words of Peter Caws, "structures are structures of systems; systems function, structures in them selves do not function — but systems function because they have the structures they do."[23]

Again, structure is not merely form. Form can be abstracted from the matter or content. For example, the form of a glass will remain unaltered whatever material may be used in making it. In contrast to form, structure is "precisely the significative (as opposed to the material) content of the system."[24]

Claude Levi-Strauss, an eminent French anthropologist, combined Marx's notion[25] of structure with De Sanssure's concept of linguistic structure for the analysis of primitive cultures and their myths. In his analysis he showed that there is no single basic myth, and all myths are transformations of the deep structure common to all societies. He compared the mythical thought to *bricolage* and the mythmaker to a *bricoleur* who builds up structures by fitting up events together, or rather the remains of events...."[26] He, in collaboration with Roman Jacobson, one of the greatest linguists of the twentieth century and founder of the Russian Formalism, analysed Baudelaire's poem "Les Chats," which became a set piece of structuralist criticism.

Gerard Genette slightly modified Levi-Strauss' concept of bricolage and bricoleur and said that the bricoleur is the critic. The critic, like the bricoleur dismantles the initial work, a structure, "into its elements — one element per card.... He, next, builds up a new structure while arranging these oddments."[27] We can say with Genette that the critic's task is structuration of the given material, the written text. For the critic the text is everything. He must not impose his own ideological prejudices on the text; on the other hand he must make it possible to uncover the connection that exists between a system of forms and a system of meanings by replacing the search for term-by-term analysis with one for overall homologues.[28]

It is not enough for him to study the structure of poetic language and of the forms of literary expression, he has also to analyse the relation between code and message.[29] Roland

Barthes expressed the same idea that the critic is not called upon to reconstitute the message of the work, but its system just as the business of the linguist is not to decipher the meaning of a sentence but to determine the formal structure which permits the transmission of its meaning.[30]

Jonathan Culler, the American structuralist has applied Chomsky's Transformational Generative Grammar for the analysis of the literary texts to understand the deep structure through the surface structure.

Finally, the structuralists and post-structuralists maintain* that literary criticism is autonomous and is to be distinguished from literary art. Literature is a discourse on reality and, therefore, uses object language, but criticism is a discourse on discourse of reality and hence its language is metalanguage. Related to this concept is the notion that a literary text is basically a linguistic structure and, therefore, the critic has to discover the reality presented in the text through linguistic analysis.

Practice. In practice the structuralists and post-structuralists are very much like the New Critics of America. But whereas the American New Critics are concerned with the "Literary" aspect only, the structuralists study a text in relation to culture and are not hesitant to read the details of its author's biography and thus take a comprehensive view of literature.

The post-structuralists make distinction between structural analysis and textual analysis. According to Barthes structural analysis is applied to oral narratives, especially myth; textual analysis, on the other hand, is applied exclusively to written narratives. Since, for every reader, certain symbols are more significant than others, textual analysis aims at "producing a mobile structuration of the text (a structuration which is displaced from reader to reader throughout history) of staying in the signifying volume of the work, in its significance." ...[It] does not try to find out what it is that determines the text (gathers it together as the end term of a causal sequence) but rather how the text explodes and disperses.[31]

---

* I have used the terms "structuralists" and "post-structuralist" because the distinction is still being made. But in my opinion the term post-structuralist is a misnomer.

As every text offers plurality of meaning, the aim is not to find the meaning but to locate and classify the form and code according to which meanings are possible. Secondly, as every text is a kind of narration, and the authorial voice is continually discernible, the technique of narratology is used for establishing the relationship between the actants and functions, the nucleus and the catalysers. Thirdly, no narration can move straight and if it does so, it will never arrest the attention of the listener/ reader nor can arouse his/her curiosity. A successful narration moves dialectically and at the end synthesises the diverse actions. Therefore, textual analysis examines the initiating event, the opposing event, the different actants and their functions, the dialectical movement and the final synthesis in the terminating event. Fourthly, a distinction has to be made between the *fabula* (story) and *sjuzet* (text) because the writer makes stylistic choices in composing the surface structure of the text. Fifthly, the technique of rhetorical analysis is used, which in the words of David Lodge, means the analysis of "the surface structure of narrative texts to show how the linguistic mediation of a story determines its meaning and effect."[32]

Finally, the text is divided into lexias, units of reading, textual signifiers for a detailed analysis and structuration.

Structuralism is more objective, scientific and comprehensive than any other theory or method of literary criticism being practised in Britain and USA. It is because of its comprehensiveness, added by theoretical assumptions and ideological implications, that it is gaining ground in the English speaking world and the day is soon to come when it will be a part of post-graduate course in all Indian universities.

(VI) DECONSTRUCTION

Jacques Derrida, chief exponent of Deconstruction, has challenged the basic assumption of the Western philosophy and classical structuralism of Claude Levi-Strauss. Through a close reading of texts he has demonstrated the contradictions in them that deconstruct their entire edifice.

In the Western philosophy there is the basic assumption that there is an order of meaning, truth, logic, logos, which serves as foundation. On the basis of this assumption philosophers have conceived meaning, essence, serious, transcendental and positive as prior or fundamental and form, accident, non-serious, empirical and negative as complication, derivation or manifestation of the first.[33] Derrida after examining the texts of the philosophers has successfully demonstrated how these hierarchical structures are subverted by the very texts and arguments they rely on them.

Derrida has attacked the two constructs of the classical structuralism; first, that literature is a discourse on reality and criticism a discourse on discourse, hence metalanguage and second that speech has primacy over writing. By a close reading of Levi-Strauss's writings Derrida has deconstructed his construct of *bricolage* and *bricoleur* and structure. He has pointed out that writing is more important because it is open to analysis but speech is not and thus deconstructs De Saussure's construct.

These undoings have far-reaching effect on literary criticism. According to Jonathan Culler, there are three important effects of Deconstruction or literary criticism.

First, by reversing and dislodging philosophical hierarchies, Deconstruction makes interpretation process of questioning, exercising and investigating the very categories on which reading depends, exploring how they are affected by the machinations of the work one is reading.

Second, Deconstruction like other theories such as Marxism, Existentialism and Feminism, identifies topics which are structural problems in literary works. These topics are the relations between speech and writing, presence and absence, simple word and metaphor, *ecriture* (mode of writing) and trace, signifier and signified and sign and free play.

Third, Deconstruction explores the peculiar, uncanny relations within texts and between texts and thus repudiates the New Critics' assumption that the conflicting emotions in a poem are resolved into a higher unity.

Fourth, according to Hillis J. Miller, a disciple of Derrida, "Deconstruction is a mode of interpretation of works by a careful and circumspect entering of each textual labyrinth" and "demonstrate that the structure of the text has already dismantled."[34]

The Technique of Deconstruction

1. Aporia. Aporia means undecidability. Contradictory meanings can be derived from the same. Derrida in his analysis of Karl Marx's *Eighteenth Brumaire of Louis Bonaparte* and Claude Levis Strauss's *The Savage Man* has amply demonstrated the contradictions in these texts and this he has done by juxtaposing the literary tropes in them.

2. There is no centre. As there are contradictions in a text, there can not be a central meaning or a centre round which the story moves. Therefore, the reader should not search the central essence of the text. Every text has two meanings : the surface meaning and the hidden meaning. Since all words are metaphorical (language has evolved from metaphors in its primary stage) the reader should remove the sediment of metaphors to discover the hidden meaning.

3. Finally, the reader should deconstruct the text, that is, s/he see should through the constructed nature of words in a text for its true interpretation.

Deconstruction has come a long way since the seventies. The feminist criticism has largely adopted its technique. Following the foundations of Derrida's philosophy, Helen Cixous has deconstructed the age old notions about women in her famous article "Sorties." The leading critics are Paul de Man, Hillis Miller, Harold Bloom, Gayatri Chakravarty Spivak and Jonathan Cullar.

Feminist Criticism

Feminist criticism has its roots in the feminist movement that began in the nineteenth century. The feminists demanded social and political rights. Earlier women were deprived of education and property rights Aphra Behn (1640-89), perhaps the first woman novelist and playwright of England, advocated for women education and wrote the book *Necessity for Women Education*. Many Wollstonecraft' *A Vindication for the Rights of Women*, J.S. Mill's *The Subjection of Women*, Virginia Woolf's *A Room of One's Own* and Simone de Beauvoir's *The Second Sex* are the books that laid the foundations of feminist criticism.

In the beginning feminist criticism was limited to :

(a) the analysis of women characters depicted by male writers and exposure of the biasness in the male point of view.

(b) the revival of women writers, neglected by male literary historians.

Thus Fielding, Smollett, Sterne and other writers were re-examined and novelists like Aphra Behn, Maria Edgeworth, Fanny Burney and others were discussed widely. But the real thrust came in the sixties when feminist criticism began to be founded on philosophical, sociological and linguistic grounds of Karl Marx, structuralism, post-structuralism and deconstruction.

At present, as Elaine Showalter, has pointed out, there are four major models in feminist criticism : (a) biological, (b) psychoanalytic, (c) linguistic and (d) cultural.

(a) Biological criticism is concerned with the woman's body. Showalter writes : "Organic or biological criticism is the most extreme statement of gender difference, of a text indelibly marked by the body : anatomy is textuality."

The leaders of this kind of criticism are Sandra Gilbert, Susan Gubar, Adrienne Rich and others. They accept the body difference between man and woman but reject the Victorian notion of woman's inferiority and Freud's psycho-analysis. Their viewpoint is that women are not inferior to men in creativity. Besides, they generally stress the importance of the body as a source of imagery.

(b) Psycho-analytic model. Psycho-analytic feminist criticism locates the difference between the psyche of men and women. The difference between biocriticism and psycho-analytic criticism is rather vague. They overlap each other. The former says that all metaphors and imagery stem from woman's body, the latter that they emanate from her psyche. The metaphors are the same. The psycho-analytic feminist critics attack Freud and Jacques Lacan. The main critics are Cora Kaplan, Anis Pratt, Joan Roberts and Ann Douglas.

(c) Sociological model. Although Showalter makes distinction between linguistic and cultural, it is difficult to agree with her taxonomy. Language is a part of culture. Therefore it is better to call this kind of feminist criticism "sociological."

Helen Cixous, Julia Kristeva, Gayatri Chakravarty Spivak, Catherine Belsey, Toril Moi and others take woman in her entirety. They question the philosophical foundations of man-woman relationship and deconstruct the age old concepts following Derrida, the writing of history from male point of view, the making of language and the gender bias and finally the place of woman in man-made society. They interpret the old texts from the woman point of view.

Elaine Showalter edited *The New Feminist Criticism* in 1985 and Toril Moi got her famous book Sexual/Textual Politics in 1985. But after fifteen years feminist criticism has got a lot of change. The influence of Marx, Roland Barthes and Jacques Derrida has made it more comprehensive and theoretically valid.

(VII) STYLISTICS

Although stylistics is not a literary theory, it is useful for researchers in the analysis of a literary text. It is very much like the "close reading" of the New Critics; the difference is that it has its base in modern linguistic and therefore, its study of literary style is more scientific. It is a method and technique, not a theory.

Definition and Theoretical Background

"Linguistics is the science of describing language and showing how it works; stylistics is that part of linguistics which concentrates on variation in the use of language, often, but not exclusively, with special attention to the most conscious and complex uses of language in literature."[35]

A linguist is concerned with the structure of language (phone, phoneme, morpheme, word, phrase, clause and sentence) and its function in society, the stylistician with choices of a writer. The stylistician, to quote Turner again,

"needs to begin with a theory of the linguistic scheme and relate it to particular speeches and writings, even if he is ultimately justified as the linguist not of our abstract competence in language but of our particular performance."[36]

Language has the property of *creativity*. It means that speakers produce such sentences that were not written or spoken before. In other words speakers and writers deviate at phonological, morphological, syntactic and semantic levels. A creative writer also deviates (of course, within the norms of tradition) from the scheme and uses variations. S/he does so to produce novelty by a creative jump. A scheme of language is never complete and static. People go on experimenting with words, phrases and syntax. Besides, new words are created and old words are given new meaning.

Literary language is different from other kinds of discourse. It establishes relationship with the scheme of core language by using linguistic elements to build new schemes of its own. In all genres of literature — literary essay, drama, poetry and novel — the writer devises his/her own way of structuring sentences, choosing words and phrases and making sound effects. Hopkins was fond of alliteration and portmanteau words. Lewis Carroll's experiments with language in *Alice in Wonderland* and *Through the Looking Glass* is well known. Shakespeare accumulated a cluster of metaphors in the highly emotional speeches of his heroes and heroines.

The creative writer's choice of vocabulary, phrase and structure defies the already existing scheme of language and gives a novelty to his/her style.

Turner writes

"The superimposition of literary schemes on the scheme of ordinary language creates a very interesting stylistic study because the two schemes are consciously played off one against the other, but the existence of multiple schemes is not in itself special to literary langage."[37]

Method and Technique of Analysis

Every creative writer follows the literary tradition and makes innovations. When s/he follows tradition s/he (a) retains the old paraphernalia of literary expression and (b) conforms with scheme of language in use in the past.

Minor writers and versifiers follow tradition without making any kind of innovation. Good writers depart from tradition and *make creative use of language.*

Stylistics studies and analyses the creative use of language; it is in the creative use of language that a writer's originality and individuality is clearly manifest. For creativity the writer makes (a) the original use of the established possibilities of language and (b) in other cases s/he goes beyond those possibilities, that is, s/he creates new communicative possibilities which are not already in the language. If we compare the essays of Bacon with those of Lamb, we will find that Lamb has made a number of deviations. Similarly Shakespeare and Milton departed from the Italian tradition of the sonnet.

There are three main levels of language : realization, form and semantics.

Realization	:	phonology (sound system)
		graphology (writing system)
Form	:	grammar and lexicon
Semantics	:	(denotative/connotative) meaning.

This three level model is applicable to both productive and receptive processes of language and the four possibilities which are :

(a) Homophony	:	Same pronunciation but different form (right-rite; night-knight; sight-site)
(b) Differentiation	:	Same form, different pronunciation (wind; minute; bow)
(c) Synonymy	:	Same meaning, different form
(d) Polysemy	:	Same form, different meaning (light, grave, dust)

The creative writer operating at these three levels and four possibilities of language departs from the tradition in the following areas.

(a) Lexis (word)

(i) Neologism, or the invention of new words.

The new words are called *nonce-formations*. Here an existing rule of word formation is applied with greater generality than customary.

Shakespeare used the word *unsex* in Macbeth on the pattern of unleash, unhorse, and Hopkins *unchilding, unfathering* deep. Similarly T.S. Eliot has used *foresuffer* on the pattern of foresee, foreknow and foretell.

(ii) Blend or Portmantean words.

Here the writer blends two words (their parts) to form a

new word. Smog, brunch and diminish are most commonly used blends in English today. Shakespeare, Milton and Hopkins have used blends for greater effect in meaning especially connotative.

(b) Grammatical Deviation

There are types of grammatical deviation. The first is deviation at the surface level and the second at the deep level. While deviating from the normal order of words and phrases in a sentence a writer lays emphasis on certain words or phrases. This is also called inversion. Milton begins *Paradise Lost* with the object of the sentence, which is not the normal way of writing. Similarly Shelley writes "Bird thou never wert" in "Ode to A Skylark." But when the word collocation is unusual and surprises us, it is deviation at the deep level. Dylan Thomas does it frequently — "a grief ago," "moonlong" "farm-yards away," Yeats has used the phrase "translunar paradise."

(c) Graphological Deviation

There is a system of printing poetry; capitalization, length of lines and metrical pattern are all regular. But poets have deviated from time to time. Hopkins's sprung rhythm, Whitman's uneven length of lines and free verse in our time are some of the examples. Some modern poets have given up the system of beginning a line of poetry with a capital letter. William Carlos Williams and E.E. Cummings are the great deviationists.

(d) Historical Deviation

A poet does not restrict himself/herself to the language of his or her period. Besides s/he may borrow words and expressions from other languages. Milton used English words in their Latin meaning. Hopkins used words of Celtic origin. In other words poets use archaic words, phrases and structures for richness of meaning and novelty of expression. Eliot has used a number of expressions from foreign languages including Sanskrit.

Apart from these, stylistics takes note of tropes like foregrounding, parallelism, repetition, metre, rhythm and the irrational in poetry.

Stylistics, though limited in scope has opened a new door

for the study of literature and helped the reader to have a better reading of a text.

POST-COLONIAL THEORY

Post-colonial theory of literature is quite recent and analyses literary texts from a new angle. Although the post-colonial critics do not name Karl Marx, they are highly influenced by his idea. Colonialism is the highest form of imperialism, said Lenin. At first came capitalism and then the expansion of the capitalist empire to the Asian and African countries. Not satisfied with gaining profit from these continents, the Europeans established colonies to exploit these people. In order to perpetuate their supremacy they established centres of Oriental studies.

After Marx, Engels, Lenin, and Gramsci, Anwar Abdel Malek criticized the European hegemony in his famous article "Orientalism in Crisis" (1963). Drawing heavily on this article, Edward Said wrote *Orientalism* (1978) which may be said to be the foundation stone of post-colonial theory of literature. Orientalism, he says, is the discourse of the West about the East; it is "a Western style for dominating, restructuring, and having authority over the Orient."

It is on this basis that post-colonial critics examine the texts written during the colonial period and those written after it. Edward Said, in his analysis of Jane Austen's *Mansfield Park*, points out the background of the cosy, ordered Mansfield Park that it is supported by an estate in Antigua. The central irony is that the order and civilization of Mansfield Park would "not have been possible without the slave trade, sugar, and the colonial planter class."

The general attitude of the European writers, barring a few, is to make distinction between the West and the East, the We and the Other. The Other is uncouth, uncivilized, dull and dependent on the We. The task of the We is to educate and civilize the Other.

Post-colonial theory is in its nascent stage, like the other two theories New-historicism and Cultural-materialism, both offshoots of Marxism, but has made a great impact on the Asian, African and the Black creative writers and critics.

However, it is difficult to agree with their interpretation of E.M. Forster and Jane Austen. The charges that have been levelled by Edward Said can be levelled against him and his semitism. The kings and emperors uptill fifteenth century attacked the neighbouring countries, won them, ruled over them and imposed their language, religion and culture. Colonialism started only after the industrial revolution and a large number of scholars had international outlook. He should read Marx, Tolstoy and Ruskin again. Dr. Douglas Hyde had advised his people to de-Anglicize Ireland and Irish literature.

REFERENCES

1. Wilbur Scott, ed., *Five Approaches of Criticism* (London and New York : Collier Macmillan, 1962).
2. *Ibid.*, 13.
3. William J. Handy and Max Westbrook, *Twentieth Century Criticism : Major Statements* (Delhi : Light and Life Publishers, 1976).
4. *Ibid.*, xii.
5. Quoted. W.K. Wimsatt and Cleanth Brooks, *Literary Criticism : A Short History* (Calcutta : Oxford Book Company 1964), 665.
6. N. Frye, "Myth, Fiction and Displacement," *Twentieth Century Criticism*, ed. Handy and Westbrook, 166.
7. *Ibid.*, 168.
8. Gilbert Murary, "Hamlet and Orestes," *Five Approaches of Library Criticism*, ed. Wilbur Scott, (Toronto : Collier-Macmillan Canada Ltd., 1962), 272.
9. Carl Jung, "Archetypes of the Collective Unconscious," *Twentieth Century Criticism*, ed. Handy & Westbrook, 205.
10. *Ibid.*, 206.
11. Carl Jung, "Psychology and Literature," *Twentieth Century Criticism : A Reader*, ed. David Lodge, 186.
12. N. Frye, *Anatomy of Criticism : Four Essays*, (Princeton, New Jersey : Princeton Univ. Press, 1956), 125.
13. Northrop Frye, "Archetypes of Literature," *Twentieth Century Criticism* ed., Handy and Westbrook, 237.
14. Northrop Frye, "Archetypes of Literature," *Twentieth Century Criticism* ed., Handy and Westbrook, 240.
15. Marx and Engels, *On Literature and Art* (Moscow : Progress Publishers, 1978), 128.
16. George Thomson, "The Art of Poetry" *Marxists on Literature*, ed., David Craig, (London: Penguin, 1973), 63.
17. Marx and Engels, *Selected Works*, (Moscow : Progress Publishers, 1969),

47-48. How the middle class after gaining economic power in the seventeenth century began to assert itself in literature is well described by L.C. Knights, *Drama and Society in the Age of Jonson.*

18. Marx and Engels, *On Literature and Art,* 90.
19. *Ibid.*, 87.
20. Man and Engels, *On Literature and Art.*
21. Arnold Kettle, "Dickens and the Popular Tradition," *Marxists on Literature,* ed., David Craig, (London : Penguin, 1973), 214.
22. Arnold Kettle, "Dickens and the Popular Tradition," *Marxists on Literature,* ed., David Craig, (London : Penguin, 1973), 214.
23. Peter Caws, "Structuralism," *Dictionary of the History of Ideas, ed.,* Philip P. Wiener, (New York : Scribner's, 1968), 322.
24. *Ibid.*, 322.
25. *Ibid.*, 326.
26. Claude Levi-Strauss, "The Science of the Concrete," *Twentieth Century Criticism,* ed., Handy and Westbrook, 446.
27. Gerard Genette, "Structuralism and Literary Criticism," *Modern Criticism and Theory,* 64.
28. *Ibid.*, 66.
29. *Ibid.*, 67.
30. Roland Barthes, "Criticism as Language," *20th Century, Criticism,* ed., David Lodge, 172.
31. Roland Barthes, "Textual Analysis : Poe's 'Valdemar,'" *Modern Criticism and Theory,* 172.
32. Jonathan Culler, "Hartman and Derrida" *Journal of Literary Criticism,* December 1984 (Delhi : Doaba House), 87-90.
33. *Ibid.*
34. Quoted by M.H. Abrams, The Deconstructive Angel" *Modern Criticism and Theory,* 272.
35. G. Turner, *Stylistics* (London : Penguin, 1970), 7.
36. *Ibid.*, 14.
37. *Ibid.*, 16.

7

The Literary Thesis

Armed with the tools and methods of research, the researcher goes to select a topic for writing an M.Phil. thesis or a doctoral dissertation. It is also expected that he will have written two or three research papers during the period of his research. It may be also that his M.Phil. thesis is an enlargement of his research paper. The research student who is going to write a research paper or a thesis must know the difference between the two because in the absence of this knowledge he will not be able to see his goal.

I

The research paper, M.Phil., thesis and doctoral dissertation are all products of research and require the same kind of labour, perseverance and sincerity; the only difference is that of range.

The Research Paper. The research paper is usually a documented article of moderate length. It is analytical, argumentative and interpretive in nature and discusses a topic limited in range. For example, the topic *The Imagery of Shakespeare's Plays* will be too wide for a research paper; it will be wise of the research student to limit it to "The imagery of *Macbeth*." Even in advanced countries like the USA, universities have come to realise the fact that a research paper should not be ambitious in scope; it should be limited in range, deep in study, moderate in length and explicate an important point. In Herbert Lehman College, University of New York, where a course is given on the methods of research and paper-writing, the earlier objective was stated thus.

"This course emphasises the writing of formal analytic essays and the basic methods of research common to various academic disciplines. Students will write frequently in and out of class. By the close of the semester, students will demonstrate mastery of the formal expository essay and the research paper."

The changed version is,

This course emphasises the writing of analytical essays and the methods of inquiry common to various academic disciplines. Students will write frequently in and out of class. By the close of the semester, students will demonstrate their ability to write essays incorporating references to suitable sources of information and to use appropriate methods of documentation.[1]

The deletion of words "mastery of the formal expository essay" from the objective is significant. What is expected from research students is consultation of the books and papers relevant to the topic and their proper documentation.

M.Phil. thesis. The M.Phil. thesis is wider in scope. The University of Cambridge expects it to be about 100 pages in size, excluding the bibliography and appendices. It is expected from the research student to demonstrate mastery of the expository essay. Since the time given for writing the M.Phil. thesis is at least six months, it is expected that the student has studied all the primary sources and a large bulk of the secondary sources and developed his own point of view. The M.Phil. thesis can be of two kinds: first, a study of a text or a comparative study of two texts similar in theme or technique; second a critical analysis of an important aspect of an author.

For a research paper the topic "The Imagery of Macbeth" will be appropriate but an M.Phil. thesis will need a wider subject. It will be better if the research student studies all the important aspects of the play. He can also make a comparative study of two texts, for example, John Steinbeck's *The Pearl* and Ernest Hemingway's *The Old Man and the Sea.* If he is more ambitious and widely read, he can take a topic like *The Image of woman in Virginia Woolf's Mrs. Dalloway and To The Lighthouse.*

Doctoral Dissertation. The doctoral dissertation is the culmination of research. Much wider in scope than the M.Phil. thesis, it makes a thorough investigation of the subject and evinces the research student's analytical, argumentative and interpretive abilities. Most of the universities expect a doctoral dissertation to be original and a genuine contribution to knowledge. However, it is difficult to define the phrase "a genuine contribution to knowledge." Since English is a foreign language and the Indian research students cannot compete with the native speakers, it is better to modify the condition and limit it to "a fresh interpretation of the known facts" and/ or "discovery of new facts." A few bright research students may make "a genuine contribution to knowledge" but a large number cannot.

The doctoral dissertation is not a book. A book on Keats or Dickens will cover all the aspects of the poet or the novelist and, therefore, will be much larger in size and scope than a doctoral dissertation which concentrates on a particular topic. *John Keats* or *Charles Dickens* : *A Critical Introduction* may be the title of a book that may contain about 300 printed pages, but the doctoral dissertation, because it studies an aspect which has been neglected till date or the facts hitherto unknown, will be shorter in size. The University of Cambridge expects a Ph.D. thesis to contain about 400 typed pages. The American universities demand a doctoral dissertation to be written in about 250 typed pages which, in my opinion, is reasonable and can be made a condition in Indian universities. A voluminous dissertation containing 700 pages or nearly so will never do justice to the subject as it will mix up too many things and may blur the main argument to justify the idiom "not to see the woods for trees."

II

Choice of the Topic. Selection of the topic is the greatest problem a research student faces in the beginning. Generally, a student approaches a supervisor for a topic. The supervisor may or may not suggest a topic. If he suggests a topic, it may be that the student is not interested in the suggested topic. It is also possible that the supervisor is not fully aware of the scope of the topic. In fact, the selection of a topic is made by the joint effort of the student and the supervisor.

How to Choose a Topic. There are two categories of students : the M.Phil. students and the Ph.D. students. The M.Phil. students are in a more advantageous position whether they are going to choose a topic for M.Phil., thesis or doctoral dissertation; they have already had a course in research methodology and learnt through discussion with their teachers how to select a topic. Besides, participation in seminars and experience of writing term papers have made their task easy. When they go to write the doctoral dissertation, they usually enlarge the scope of the topic on which they have already written the M.Phil. thesis. The same advantage is enjoyed by those research students who have successfully completed pre-Ph.D. course.

The students who have had no such course are like wanderers without a compass in a large lake. They do not know what they should do first. Naturally, they approach a teacher and request him to suggest a topic. They do not know that a teacher is not an encyclopaedia of English literature and without their co-operation he cannot help them. Research students are advised to follow these steps for the selection of a topic so that they can save time and energy.

(i) Study of the complete works of the author. In M.A. no student can read all the works of the authors prescribed in the course. Generally only one work of an author is prescribed and a student studies that work and a few critical works on it. Naturally, his knowledge is confined to the text prescribed. But this knowledge will not help him much in his research. He can have a full view of the author when he studies all his works. It has been seen that an author's autobiography, letters, journals and critical writings have helped us more in comprehending his creative works than the commentaries and critical studies.

(ii) Study of a few standard critical studies. After the study of the primary sources, the research student should read the critical studies on the author. This will help him understand the texts and the author's thought better and give him the opportunity to compare his view with those of the other scholars and critics and also, more importantly, know the neglected aspects of the author, which in his opinion, are important and worth discussion.

(iii) Narrowing the topic to specificity. The final step is to narrow the topic chosen. Suppose a student has studied the complete works of W.B. Yeats and a few critical books on him. Now he decides the topic *A Critical Study of W.B. Yeats's Poetry.*

He feels elated that he has selected only one aspect of Yeats's total works. But this topic is too wide. It can be the title of a book, not a doctoral dissertation.

When he is told that the topic is wide, he makes another effort and narrows it to *Myths in the Poetry of W.B. Yeats.* The topic now is limited and the research student can make a deep study of myths in general and Yeats's use of them in his poetry. But this topic, too, is wide. The student shall have to study Greek mythology, Irish mythology and Indian mythology thoroughly. Perhaps it will take years for him in finding and collecting materials. Therefore, it will be wise for him to narrow the topic further to *Irish Mythology in the Poetry of W.B. Yeats.*

Now it will be possible for him to make a deep study of the Irish myths. He will also be able to explain how far Yeats was successful in using them in his poetry. The study will be deep, penetrating and illuminating.

Finally, the research student must know that no topic is good or bad in itself. A topic which may seem brilliant and interesting in the beginning may not be worth-pursuing and a topic which appeared dull at first may prove really interesting and worth study.

Scholars have formulated certain criteria for the selection of a topic.

Criteria for Selection of a Topic

(i) Adequate supervision. A research student must make it sure that the supervisor he is going to choose is an expert in the field of his research. If the student wants to study an American author and the supervisor is an expert in British literature, he will not benefit by his supervisor's knowledge. The second important point to consider is whether the supervisor is in a position to spend sufficient time to the student Generally, heads of departments, deans of faculties and principals of colleges, being engaged in administrative work, do not have required time to give to their research student. A colleague of mine after becoming vice chancellor could not spare even three days for his M.Phil. and Ph.D. students for three years! Since the advice of the supervisor is of immense value to the student, it is necessary that they should often meet and discuss the specific problems that continually arise during research.

(ii) Interest in the topic. By this we do not mean that the topic should be interesting. What is meant here is that the research student takes interest in the topic. But how will he take interest in the topic? Psychologists say that we take interest in those things of which we have prior knowledge and do those things which are easy for us. Technically speaking, we continue a work only when there is reinforcement. We can apply the findings of Skinner's operant conditioning here too. For the creation of interest, it is necessary that the student should read widely all the works by the author and a few books of criticism. Once he has read them and enjoyed them, he will develop his interest in the author and his age. This knowledge will help him in future too as he will find it easy to understand the points of view of other critics and evolve his own viewpoint.

(iii) Time factor. As said earlier, there is a difference between a book and a doctoral dissertation. A book is the result of long teaching experience or the revision of doctoral dissertation. Naturally, it takes a longer time to write. The time allotted for a doctoral dissertation is usually *five* years. The universities where students have to do M.Phil. or undergo the pre-Ph.D. course, the total time for writing is reduced to two and a half years. Within this period, the researcher has to prepare the tentative bibliography, collect materials, take notes, make arrangement of the collected data, write three drafts of the dissertation, get it typed and send it to a printer for printing the title and cover page. All these are time consuming especially for the reason that the field of investigation is almost new to both the student and the supervisor.

The subject selected, therefore, should be such as can be completed within the given length of time. If the student cannot be reasonably certain that the subject in question can be finished in the given time limit, he must either choose another subject or race against time. The second aspect of time element is that the topic should not be too narrow and limited. If a thesis can be completed within six month's time, it will be at best an M.Phil. thesis, not a doctoral dissertation.

(iv) Library facilities. Library facilities are essential for literary research. The student before selecting the topic must make it sure that the library nearest to the centre of research can provide him with the most essential books and journals. It is certain that no library contains all the books published and the researcher has to consult many libraries to collect materials. However, he expects that the library contains the most important books he needs. He can go to other libraries for supplementary reading. If it is not so, he will have to spend considerable time, energy and money to find materials and it may be that even after his best efforts he has not been able to read the books listed in the tentative bibliography.

Related to it is the availability of books. The supervisor should also make it sure if sufficient materials are available in different libraries. There are a few British authors on whom critical books are scant. A student in consultation with his supervisor decided to do research on Somerset Maugham. He could easily find out the novels but to his great dismay he could not get even a single full-length study of Maugham. After one and half year he gave up the project. The other student faced the same problem when his supervisor advised him to study James Barry, the playwright. She, inspite of all her efforts, could not read all the plays within the stipulated period and her search for critical books proved abortive.

(v) New area of investigation. Before starting to work on a subject the supervisor and the student must make it sure that what is being proposed to be studied has not been done already. The Academic and Research section of every university possesses a list of the titles of the doctoral dissertations. On request, the dealing assistant gives the list to the student. Now the UGC has started publishing the titles of doctoral dissertations submitted at different universities.

In case, someone decides to do research on the topic already done, he must give reasons why he is doing so. It may be that new facts have been discovered or that the previous research was faulty in its methods and hence erroneous in conclusion.

(vi) Dead authors or living authors. Earlier research degree committees did not allow research students to do research on living authors. Now they have revised their stand and allow students to study the living authors like Edward Albee, Arnold Wesker, Harold Pinter, William Golding and many other established poets, dramatists and novelists. However, there is always a confusion.

The great danger with living authors is that many of them are still writing and there are very few full-length studies on them. In the first case, it is possible that when the research student has got his dissertation typed and bound, two recent books of the author have appeared in the market. The non-availability of critical books is a serious handicap. One cannot rely solely on reviews and critical introductions. The research students who had started doing research on D.J. Enright, Elizabeth Jennings, Elizabeth Bowen, Edward Bond, Thornton Wilder, Anita Desai and many like these had to abandon their project only because they did not find sufficient critical materials.

It is therefore advisable that if living authors are chosen at all, the supervisor and the candidate must make it sure that he or she is at the fag end of his or her literary career and there is little possibility of the production of a new book.

(vii) Feasibility. The final consideration is the value and importance of the results achieved. This is not to say that all these and especially the M.Phil. theses must represent "discoveries," original and strikingly important contributions to knowledge; what is significant is that the study must be relevant to the needs of society. The research student and his/her supervisor must know that the dissertation shall be placed in the university library and be read by other students. If the topic is such as would not attract the attention of the future research students, the whole labour of four to five years is fruitless. It is also to be noted that the topic should be able to attract the attention of the publishers also. The test of a good dissertation is its publication in the book form and popularity among readers.

III

A. Planning the Research Programme

After the selection of the topic, the next step is planning the research programme. Without a plan the research student cannot decide what things to do first. In fact, action without planning is blind. While writing a research paper or a thesis the student is given plenty of time to plan and organise his work. He is given the opportunity to read widely, collect materials sufficiently, take notes systematically, arrange his thoughts logically and commit them to paper in an acceptable way. A much higher quality of work is expected of him.

While it is true that a student writing a thesis or doctoral dissertation may be given advice from time to time by his supervisor, the ultimate responsibility is his. For any fault in the format of the thesis, organisation of thought and delay in submission he will be blamed. Consequently, once he starts reading around the topic and collecting materials for it, he soon comes to realise that he has to read extensively and write considerably. He cannot omit important information nor leave out the essential details nor present only part of the evidence. It is, therefore, necessary that he should follow a time schedule. The total programme should be planned in an order that it can be completed in the time allotted. The failure to schedule time usually results in an inferior product.

A suggested allocation of time is as follows :

(i)	Defining and limiting problem, consulting source material and collecting information	50%	15 months
(ii)	First draft	30%	9 months
(iii)	Second draft including footnotes referencing and revision of the first draft	10%	3 months
(iv)	Final draft adding further information and revision of language	5%	1½ month
(v)	Typing and binding (proof-reading included)	5%	1½ month

The researcher may adjust the time allocation according to his convenience.

B. Format of a Thesis/Doctoral Dissertation

Every thesis has a beginning, a middle and an end. The researcher while writing a thesis must show the development of ideas through successive stages. He has also to explain the purpose of research, its usefulness and the methods adopted in his investigation. The most common format of a thesis is as follows :

(i) Preface
(ii) Table of Contents
(iii) Introduction
(iv) Main Body of the Thesis
(v) Conclusion
(vi) Appendix
(vii) Footnotes
(viii) Bibliography

(i) Preface. In the Preface the research student writes the purpose of the thesis and its usefulness. He also makes acknowledgement to different sources from where he has received help. The preface is usually short and hardly covers three pages. At the end the researcher puts his signature, place and date.

(ii) Table of Contents. After the preface there is the table of contents that contains the break up of the thesis into its several parts, *i.e.*, introduction, the chapters, conclusion, appendix and bibliography, indicating the pagination.

(iii) Introduction. The introduction is basically the survey of literature. Here the researcher discusses in brief the problem, the works done in the past by different scholars, their merits and drawbacks and his own hypothesis. The introduction may be numbered as a chapter but what is important is that it should function as an uher to the main body of the thesis.

(iv) The Chapters. The chapters form the main body of the thesis and contain the arguments, evidence and the sources of information given in the footnotes. There is no definite number of chapters but it is the usual practice to divide a thesis into

3-4 chapters of short length (say, 25 typed pages) and a doctoral dissertation into 5-6 chapters of standard length (say, 35-40 typed pages).

(v) **Conclusion.** The conclusion is usually short (10-12 typed pages). It must summarise the arguments of the chapters, modify the hypothesis made in the Introduction (though it is not always necessary), state the conclusion arrived at on the basis of evidence and, finally, evaluate the merit of the text or the author or the age. The conclusion as far as possible should be free from footnotes and quotations.

(vi) **Appendix.** The Appendix includes a brief discussion of some of the points that could not be discussed in the main body of thesis, tables and plates. Nowadays tables and plates are included in the main body of the thesis.

(vii) **Footnotes.** Footnotes, unless specially instructed, should be in the main body of the thesis, they should occur in the page where the quotation is cited or the source is referred to.

(viii) **Bibliography.** The Bibliography is always at the end of the thesis. It contains the list of the books and articles in the journals the researcher has consulted. While preparing the bibliography the research student must not miss the recent books on the subject, otherwise his thesis/dissertation will apparently look outdated and, in most cases, it is actually outdated in such a case.

Besides these, the thesis/doctoral dissertation must bear the title, name of the degree for which it is submitted, name of the supervisor with designation, name of the candidate, the university and the year of submission. The first page of the thesis/dissertation should replicate the cover page and should be followed by a certificate from the supervisor that it is the own work of the candidate and is fit for submission in accordance with the provisions of the statutes of the university.

All the pages of the thesis/dissertation must be numbered.

IV

A. Thesis Writing

The art of thesis writing is to learn by practice. The students who have been given instructions in the class how to write a research paper or a term paper are certainly in a more advantageous position, but even they find it difficult to write a thesis and this is because it is wider in scope and larger in size and demands a good command of English language. By command of English language we do not mean mastery over the register of literary English only but also of the register of social sciences. It is also important that the research student should know the difference between the style of an article in a magazine and that of a research paper or a thesis. An article in a magazine is not always exact in referring to the sources of quotations, presentation of facts and distinction between the primary sources and the secondary sources and is more subjective in its approach to the subject.

The research paper or the thesis demands objectivity, balanced views, exact reference to sources and presentation of facts. In order that his thesis or paper can be acceptable to scholars, the research student has to take note of the following:

(a) Plagiarism

(b) Style

(c) Citation

(d) Documentation

(a) Plagiarism. Plagiarism is borrowing the ideas of others without acknowledging them. If a student incorporates a few lines of a writer and does not acknowledge him, he commits plagiarism. Even when he paraphrases the ideas of others, he can be charged with plagiarism.

Plagiarism is a vice that tempts us all. The first reason is to show before others our ingenuity, brilliance and novelty. We steal the ideas of others and claim them to be our own only with the intention of concealing our weaknesses and deficiencies and exhibiting before others those qualities which we actually do not possess. The second reason, and this is mostly with the research students, is laziness and weak language. Many research students simply copy paragraphs of critical books. They do so because they do not want to paraphrase them and make acknowledgement. Sometimes verbatim long quotations without quotation marks are cited pages together only for the reason that the student cannot paraphrase them in his own words.

In all cases plagiarism must be avoided. The research student who plagiarises in his attempt to deceive others deceives himself/herself.

(b) Style. As said earlier, a research paper or a thesis is analytical and argumentative and therefore, its style will considerably differ from that of an average essay. The most important words the student has to learn are conjunctions and adverbs. Conjunctions and adverbs function as both connectives and modifiers. It will be of immense help to students if they know the use of the following conjunctions and adverbs :

(i) and, but, therefore, so, as well as, in spite of, however, nevertheless, moreover, besides, in addition to, howsoever, nonetheless, of course.

(ii) likely, partly, largely, mostly, precisely, wrongly possibly, probably, brilliantly, succinctly, aptly.

It is better to avoid the use of the personal pronoun *I* as far as possible. The research student should use the plural form *We* if he wants to use it at all. However, in the case of expressing his personal opinion or while refuting an authority he can use the personal pronoun *I*.

Eminent writers must not be referred to with an honorific. It would be improper to add Mr. before the name of T.S. Eliot or Professor before Cleanth Brooks or Northrop Frye. Similarly Miss. or Mrs. or Ms. should not be used with the names of women writers.

Finally, a research paper or thesis is a formal piece of writing. Therefore, slangs, colloquial words and expressions are to be avoided. Even contractions live won't, shouldn't, I'll or he's are not permitted unless they are a part of a quotation from a novel or play or poem. The sentences should be balanced, short and precise in expression.

(c) Citation. While quoting lines from the primary or secondary sources it has to be taken notice that the passage is quoted without any alteration or addition. If the passage quoted is not more than four typed lines it should be incorporated in the text and be indicated by quotation marks. If the passage is of more than four lines it should be an independent paragraph without quotation marks. In citation we use slash, ellipsis, sic and italics for clarity.

(i) *Slash* (/) : Slash is used when we quote lines from a poem and want to indicate the beginning and the end of the second, third or fourth line. For example, "A slumber did my spirit seal/I had no human fears/she seemed a thing that could not feel/The touch of earthly years."

(ii) *Ellipsis* : Ellipsis is used to make it clear that some words are omitted from the quoted passage. If words are omitted in the middle, we indicate the omission by three *dots*. For example, Inscape in poetry is further explained by Hopkins himself : it is "the essential only lasting thing...species or individuality — distinctive beauty of style."

If the passage quoted is a long one and a sentence or the beginning or ending part of a sentence is omitted, four dots are put to indicate that the sentence has ended somewhere. For example.

Do you know, a horrible thing has happened to me. I have begun to doubt Tennyson.... I cannot tell you how amused and I must say pleased by and comforted by this coincidence I am. A little explanation first. You know I do not mistrust my judgment as soon as you do; I say it to the praise of your modesty.

(iii) *Sic.* : The Latin word means "so." If the words quoted from the source are misspelt or wrongly used or the entire expression is faulty, we write the word *sic* in brackets to show that the fault is in the source or the quoted passage.

(iv) *Italics* : Sometimes we need to emphasise the importance of a word, a phrase or an expression. We show this by underlining or italicising it. For example, Hopkins divides poetry into three categories : Inspiration, Parnassian and Castalion. Since the word Parnassian is important, he writes it in italics. "The second kind I call *Parnassian*."

(v) *Parenthesis* : Sometimes the quoted passage is not clear because of the use of personal pronouns. It is also occasionally not clear when ellipsis is used, in such cases we add words of our own to make the passage clear. The added words are put within square brackets. The following examples will show how to make use of parentheses.

(a) "I [Hopkins] think then the language of verse may be divided into three kinds."

(b) He [Hopkins] invites imitation because he uses a large number of highly effective poetic and rhetorical devices, any one or more of which can be imitated;

(c) All sounds, all colours, all forms, either because of long association, evoke indefinable and yet precise emotions [and] call down among us certain disembodied powers...."

(d) *Documentation* : Documentation is recording the exact sources of information. The writer of an article in a magazine need not refer to the source of a quotation or an idea but the researcher, because his task is serious, must refer to the exact sources of information so that other can consult them if they feel the need to do so.

Documentation has two aspects : footnotes and bibliography. Footnotes unless otherwise specified should be incorporated in the main body of the text. Bibliography is the list of books consulted by the researcher. Bibliography is of there kinds (a) General Bibliography (b) Selected Bibliography and (c) Annotated Bibliography. Writing the General Bibliography is a kind of research which aims at recording all the primary, secondary and tertiary sources. Since a researcher cannot record all the primary and secondary sources, he usually is selective in recording the sources. Annotated Bibliography is usually appended at the end of books that introduce a subject or author to the beginners. Here, the author lists a few books and comments on their quality and usefulness to the reader. The systems of footnotes and bibliography differ in minor details.

(i) Footnotes. The general system for first reference is to write the author's name in normal order followed by a comma, then the title of the book underlined followed by a comma. After the title of the book follow place/places of publication, colon, name of the publisher, comma and the year of publication all within brackets and after the brackets page number(s).

Northrop Frye, *Anatomy of Criticism* : *Four Essays* (Princeton: Princeton Univ. Press, 1957), 55.

If the source referred to is an article in an edited book or a journal, the article is put within inverted commas :

H. Adams, "Yeats's Dialectic and Criticism," *Criticism* Vol. X, No. 3, 1962, 185-86.

If the referred source is an edited book, we write ed. after the name of the editor and even if there are two editors or more we write ed.

J. Unterecker, ed., *Yeats : A collection of Critical Essays,* (New Jersey: Prentice Hall, 1963), 51.

A.N. Jeffares and K.G.W. Cross, eds. *In Excited Reverie,* (London: Macmillan, 1965), 77.

An article in encyclopaedia is referred thus :

Author's name, title of the article, title of the encyclopaedia, Vol. No. and page number.

For subsequent references, it is enough to write the name of the author, the title of the book and page number. If the reference is to the primary sources the title of the book and page number will be enough.

The system of Bibliography is slightly different. The author's or editor's name begins with the surname followed by a full stop. The title of the book is underlined and followed by a full stop. Then follows the place of publication, a colon, name of the publisher, a comma and year of publication.

Frye, Northrop. *Anatomy of Criticism : Four Essays.* Princeton: Princeton Univ. Press, 1957.

If there are two or three authors, the first author's name begins with his surname and the other name(s) in normal order.

Wimsatt, W.K. Jr. and Cleanth Brooks. *Literary Criticism : A Short History.* London : Routledge and Kegan Paul, 1957.

If there are more than three authors the usual practice is to write the name of the first author and add *et al.* for the rest.

Quirk, Randolph *et al.*, A Grammar of *Contemporary English.* London : Longman, 1977.

For articles in journals and encyclopaedias we follow the same procedure as we do in the case of footnotes with the difference that the author's name begins with his surname.

Adams, H. "Yeats's Dialectic and Criticism," *Criticism* Vol. X, No. 3, 1962.

Abrams, M.H., "The Deconstructive Angel." *Modern Criticism and Theory,* ed. David Lodge. London : Longman 1988.

Research students are advised to study *MLA Handbook for the Writers of Research Papers* for further knowledge of documentation.

When all said and done the research student must bear in mind that neither the quality of the paper nor electronic printing nor attractive cover is of much use. What is more important is the quality of content, exactness of reference, and flawless language of the thesis or doctoral dissertation. It is diligence and interpretation of facts that come first in the writing of a thesis.

NOTE

1. Quoted. Richard L. Larsen, "The Research Paper in the Writing Course : A Non-Form of Writing," *College English* Vol. 44, No. 8 December 1982, 811.

Bibliographical References

It has been found that most of M.A., M.Phil. and Ph.D. students do not have an idea of standard books which are basic for study and research. A small classified list of these books and journals is given for their guidance.

BIBLIOGRAPHIES

Cambridge Bibliography of English Literature.

Dyson, A.E. ed., *The English Novel.* Oxford University Press.

—.*The English Poetry.* Oxford University Press.

[A.E. Dyson's *The English Novel* and *The English Poetry* give a short introduction to the authors selected and a detailed bibliography on each of them].

Sambamurthy, *V.*, Indira. *An Annotated Bibliography* of *Indian English Fiction* Delhi : Atlantic Publishers and Distributors, 2002.

Bowker, R.R. *Books in Print.*
(It is available in every standard library and contains books by and on authors, currently available in market).

Bulletins and catalogues published by standard companies.

New Arrivals in university and public libraries.

LITERARY HISTORY – BRITISH

Baugh, A.C. ed., *A Literary History of England.*

Daiches, David. *A Critical History of English Literature.*

Dobree, B. and Norman Levis. Gen. ed., *Oxford History of English Literature.*

Ford, Boris, ed. *New Pelican Guide to English Literature* 8 Vols.

Legouis, E. and Louis Cazamian. *A History of English Literature* London : JM Dent 1960.

RESEARCH METHODS

Altick, Richard D. *The Art of Literary Research*, New York : W.W. Norton Company, 1963.

Bowers, Fredson. *Bibliography and Textual Criticism*. Oxford : Clarendon Press, 1964.

Gaskell, Philip. *From Writer to Reader: Studies in Editorial Method.* Oxford : The Clarendon Press 1978.

Leavis, F.R. *English Literature in Our Time and the University.* London : Cambridge University Press, 1967.

Thorpe, James. ed. *Aims and Methods of Literary Scholarship.* Hyderabad : American Studies Research Centre, 1970.

Sanders, Chauncey. *An Introduction to Research in Literary History.* New York : Macmillan, 1957.

Wellek Rene and Alvaro Rebeiro ed. *Evidence in Literary Scholarship.* Oxford : Clarendon Press, 1979.

LITERARY CRITICISM

(a) Histories

Abrams, M.H. *The Mirror and the Lamp.* New York : Oxford University Press, 1953.

Atkins, JWH. *English Literary Criticism*, Vol. I-IV. London : Methuen, 1951.

——.*Literary Criticism in Antiquity,* Vol. I & II. Cambridge : Cambridge University Press, 1934.

The Cambridge History of Literary Criticism. Cambridge University Press, 2002.

Wellek, Rene. *A History of Modern Criticism* Vol. I-VII.

(b) Modern Critical Theories : Anthologies

Coyle, Martin *et al.* ed. *Encyclopaedia of Literature and Criticism.* London : Routledge, 1990.

Handy, WJ and Max Westbrook ed. *Twentieth Century Criticism Major Statements.* Delhi : Light and Life Publishers, 1976.

Lodge, David. *20th Century Criticism : A Reader.* London : Longman, 1972.

——.*Modern Criticism and Theory.* London : Longman, 1988.

Lucy, Niall. ed. *Postmodern Literary Theory : An Anthology.* Indian rpt. Delhi : Atlantic Publishers, 2002.

Rivkin, Julie and Michael Ryan. ed. *Literary Theory : An Anthology,* rev. edn. Indian rpt. Delhi; Atlantic Publishers and Distributors, 2002.

Scott, Wilbur ed. *Five Approaches of Literary Criticism*, Toronto : Collier-Macmillan Canada Ltd., 1962.

Sedden, Raman ed. *The Theory of Criticism*. London : Longman 1988.

(c) Modern Critical Theories : Introductions

Barry, Peter. *Beginning Theory*, 2nd edn. Manchester : Manchester University Press, 2002.

Bertens, Hans. *Literary Theory* : *The Basics*. London : Routledge 1995 Delhi: Foundation.

Chandra, NDR. ed. *Modern Literary Criticism* : *Theory and Practice*, Delhi : Authors Press, 2003.

Krishnaswamy, N. John Verghese and Sunita Misra. *Contemporary Literary Theory*. Delhi : Macmillan India, 2001.

Nayar, Pramod K. *Literary Theory Today*. Delhi : Asia Book Club, 2002.

Ray, Mohit K. *Perspectives on Criticism*. Delhi : Atlantic Publishers and Distributors, 2002.

Ryan, Michael. *Literary Theory* : *A Practical Introduction*. Indian rpt. Delhi : Atlantic Publishers and Distributors, 2002.

Webster Roger. *Studying Literary Theory* : *An Introduction* 2nd edn. London : Arnold, 1990.

(d) Forms of Literature

Abrams, M.H. *A Glossary of Literary Terms*. New York : Harcourt Brace & Company. Indian rpt. Bangalore. Prism Books Private Ltd.

Beardsley, Monroe C. Robert B. Daniel and Glen Legget. *Theme and Form* : *An Introduction to Literature* 4th ed. New Jersey : Prentice Hall, 1975.

Boulton, Marjorie. Cuddon, John A. *Anatomy of the Novel, Anatomy of Poetry, Anatomy of the Drama, A Dictionary of Literary Terms*. London : Andre Deutsch, Rev. edn. 1979.

Jump, J. *The Critical Idiom*. London : Methuen

(It is a series of books on genres and forms of literature published in different years)

Prasad, B. *A Background to The Study of Literature*. Delhi : Macmillan, 1999.

(e) Companions and guides

The companions are for individual authors, except *Oxford Companion to Literature.* The guides give a brief introduction to famous authors, texts and literary terms.

(i) *Cambridge Companion to Authors.* Delhi : Foundation.

Harvey, Pual. *Oxford Companion to Classical Literature.* Oxford : Oxford University Press.

—. *Oxford Companion to Classical Literature.* Oxford : Oxford University Press.

Ousby, Ian. ed. *Cambridge Guide to Literature.* Delhi : Foundation.

Southam, B.C. ed. *The Critical Heritage.* London : Routledge.

(This series is a collection of critical articles and reviews on different authors, not easily available, published from time to time and still in progress).

Ward, AC. *Longman Companion to English Literature.* London : Longman.

(f) Linguistics

Since post-sixties criticism and Russian Formalism are heavily influenced by linguistics, the researcher should consult the books listed here.

Crystal, David. *A Dictionary of Linguistics and Phonetics.* 5th edn. Delhi : Atlantic Publishers and Distributors, 2003.

Trask, R.L. *Language : The Basics.* London: Routledge, India. Second Edition. Delhi : Foundation, 2003.

(g) Grammar and Mechanism of Writing

GRAMMAR

Harris, Muriel. ed. *The Prentice Hall Guide to Grammar and Usage.* New Jersey : Prentice Hall, 1986.

Koch, Rachel Spack. *Focus on Grammar.* London : Longman, 2000.

Quirk, R. *et al. A Grammar of Contemporary English.* London : Longman, 1970.

MECHANISM OF WRITING

Corder, Jim W. *Contemporary Writing : Process and Practice.* Dallas Texas, Scott Foreman & Company, 1979.

Gorrell, Robert M. and Charlton Laird. *Modern English Handbook*. New Jersey : Prentice Hall, 1976.

Marius, Richard and Harvey S. Weimer. *The McGraw Hill College Handbook*. Second ed. New York : McGraw Hill, 1988.

O'Hare, Frank and Dean Memering. *The Writer's Work*. New Jersey : Prentice Hall, 1990.

AMERICAN LITERATURE

Aiken, C.P. *Twentieth Century American Poetry*. New York : Modern Library, 1944.

Bercovitch, Sacvan. *The Cambridge History of American Literature*. Cambridge University Press, 2002.

Boym, Max I. *A History of Literary Aesthetics in America*. New York : Frederick Ungar Publishing Company, 1973.

Davidson, Cathy N. and Linda Wagner Martin. ed-in-chief. *The Oxford Companion to Women's Writing in the United States*. New York : Oxford University Press, 1995.

Davidson, Marshall B. *et al*. *The American Heritage History of the Writers of America*. New York : McGraw Hill Book Company, 1973.

Hennig, Cohen. ed. *Landmarks of American Writing*. Voice of American Forum Lectures, 1969.

Perkins, Georg. ed. *American Poetic Theory*. New York : Holt, Rinehart and Winston, 1972.

Rosenthal, ML. *Modern Poets*. New York : Oxford, 1965.

—. *New Poets*. New York : Oxford, 1967.

Spiller, R. *et al*. *A Literary History of America*, New York : Oxford, 1976.

Wright, George T. *Seven American Stylists from Poe to Mailer*, Minneapolis : University of Minnesota, 1973.

INDIAN ENGLISH LITERATURE

(a) General and Cultural Histories

Antanova, K., G. Bongard-Levin and G. Kotovsky. *A History of India*. Moscow : Progress Publishers, 1979.

Basham, A.L. *The Wonder That Was India*. Delhi : Rupa, 1964, 1998.

Chattopadhyay, Gautam, ed. *Awakening in the Early Nineteenth Century*. Calcutta, 1965.

Dayal, Raghubir. *An Outline of Indian History and Culture*. Delhi : Orient Longman, 1995.

Forbes, Geraldine. *The New Cambridge History of India*. Delhi : Foundation (CUP), 1996.

Ghose, Aurobindo. *The Renaissance in India*. Pondicherry : Sri Aurobindo Ashram, 1951.

Majumdar, R.C., H.C. Raichoudhury and Kalikinkar Dutta. *An Advanced History of India*. Delhi : Macmillan, 1962.

Majumdar, R.C. *British Paramountcy and Indian Renaissance*. Bombay : Bharatiya Vidya Bhavan, 1981.

Sen, Shailendranath. *A History of Modern India* (1765-1950). Delhi : Wiley Eastern, 1986.

(b) Literary Histories and Surveys

Bhatnagar, K.C. *Realism in the Major Indo-Anglian Fiction*. Bareilly, Prakash Book Depot, 1980.

Bhatnagar, M.K. *Modern Indian English Novel*. Delhi : Atlantic Publishers and Distributors, 2003.

Clark, T.W. *The Novel in India*. London : George Allen & Unwin, 1970.

Dwivedi, A.N. *Papers on Indian Writing in English*. Delhi : Atlantic Publishers and Distributors, 2002.

Ghose, Sisir Kumar. *Makers of Indian Literature*. Delhi : Sahitya Akademy, 1986.

Iyengar, K.R.S. *Indian Writing in English*. Delhi : Sterling Publication, 1962.

Maheshwari, Vinod Kumar, *Perspectives on Indian English Literature*, Delhi : Atlantic Publishers and Distributors, 2002.

Mukherjee, Meenakshi. *The Twice Born Fiction : Themes* and *Techniques of Indian Novels in English*. Delhi : Arnold Heinmann, 1971.

Naik, M.K. *A History of Indian English Literature*. Delhi : Sahitya Akademy, 1982.

Naik, M.K. and Shyamla A. Narayan. *Indian English Literature : 1980-2000*. Delhi : Pencraft International, 2001.

Pathak, R.S. *Indian Fiction of the Nineties.* Delhi : Creative Books, 1997.

Rao, A.S. *Myth and History in Contemporary Indian Novel in English.* Delhi : Atlantic Publishers and Distributors, 2000.

Saha, Subhash Chandra. *Contemporary Indian Renaissance and Indian English Poetry.* Delhi : Prestige Books, 2000.

Verma, K.D. *The Indian Imagination.* London : Macmillan, 2000.

Vishwanathan, Gauri. *Masks of Conquest : Literary Study and British Rule in India.* London: Faber, 1990.

ANTHOLOGIES AND COMPILATIONS

Bhatnagar, M.K. ed. *Encyclopaedia of Literature in English.* Delhi : Atlantic Publishers and Distributors, 2003.

Dhawan, R.K. ed. *Indian Women Novelists,* Vol. 18 Delhi : Prestige Books, 2000.

Naikar, Basavaraj ed. *Indian English Literature,* Vol. 4 Delhi : Atlantic Publishers and Distributors, 2003.

Ray, Mohit K. ed. *Studies in Literature in English,* Vol. 6 Delhi : Atlantic Publishers and Distributors, 2003.

REPUTED JOURNALS

(a) British and American

College English. US Embassy.

Modern Fiction Studies. The John Hopkins University, USA.

Modern Language Review. Modern Humanities Research Centre, London.

New Literary Theory. The John Hopkins University.

Notes and Queries.

PMLA.

Sewanee Review.

Shakespeare Quarterly. Folger Shakespeare Library. The John Hopkins University.

Studies in Romanticism. Boston University.

Studies in The Library Imagination. Georgia State University.

Times Literary Supplement.

Victorian Fiction.

Victorian Poetry.

Yeats Annual.

(b) Indian

Aligarh Muslim University Journal of English Studies.

Indian Journal of American Studies.

Indian Journal of English Studies.

Focus on English. British Council, Chennai.

The Atlantic Critical Review. Atlantic Publishers and Distributors, New Delhi.

The Atlantic Literary Review. Atlantic Publishers and Distributors, New Delhi.

There are many other Indian journals but they are not regular.

At present, a number of standard books are available on line. The biggest publisher is Chadyck-Healey and the title is *Literature online version* 2.0. Besides, Gale is selling books on CDs. A large number of texts are available on CD-ROM. Researchers can contact the computerised libraries.